Asian Flavors

Publications International, Ltd.

Louis Weber, CEO
Publications International, Ltd.
8140 Lehigh Ave
Morton Grove, IL 60053

Pictured on the front cover: Kung Pao Chicken *(page 56).*

Pictured on the back cover *(clockwise from top left):* Ginger Tofu Bowl *(page 114),* Crab Rangoon with Spicy Dipping Sauce *(page 8),* Thai Chicken Pizza *(page 186),* Asian Lettuce Wraps *(page 6)* and Jap Chae (Korean Glass Noodle Stir-Fry) *(page 126).*

ISBN: 978-1-63938-548-5

Manufactured in China.

8 7 6 5 4 3 2 1

Table of Contents

Appetizers & Drinks

Spicy Crispy Shrimp

makes 4 servings

Sauce

- ½ **cup mayonnaise**
- 4 **teaspoons Thai chili sauce**
- 1 **teaspoon honey**
- ½ **teaspoon rice vinegar**

Shrimp

- ¾ **cup buttermilk**
- 1 **egg**
- ¾ **cup all-purpose flour**
- ½ **cup panko bread crumbs**
- 1 **teaspoon salt**
- ½ **teaspoon ground sage**
- ½ **teaspoon black pepper**
- ¼ **teaspoon onion powder**
- ¼ **teaspoon garlic powder**
- ¼ **teaspoon dried basil**
- 16 **to 20 large raw shrimp, peeled, deveined and patted dry**
- **Vegetable oil for frying**
- 2 **green onions, thinly sliced (optional)**

1. For sauce, combine mayonnaise, chili sauce, honey and vinegar in small bowl; mix well. Cover and refrigerate until ready to serve.
2. Whisk buttermilk and egg in medium bowl until well blended. Combine flour, panko, salt, sage, pepper, onion powder, garlic powder and basil in another medium bowl; mix well. Dip each shrimp in buttermilk mixture, then in flour mixture, turning to coat completely. Place breaded shrimp on large plate; refrigerate until oil is hot.
3. Heat 2 inches of oil in large saucepan over medium-high heat to 350°F; adjust heat to maintain temperature during frying. Cook shrimp in batches 2 to 3 minutes or until golden brown, turning once. Drain on paper towel-lined plate.
4. Remove shrimp to large bowl; add sauce and toss gently to coat. Garnish with green onions.

Asian Lettuce Wraps

makes 10 to 12 wraps

- **2 teaspoons peanut or vegetable oil**
- **1½ pounds boneless skinless chicken breasts or pork shoulder, cut into ¼-inch pieces**
- **2 leeks, white and light green parts chopped**
- **1 cup shiitake mushrooms, stemmed, caps chopped**
- **1 stalk celery, chopped**
- **2 tablespoons water**
- **1 tablespoon oyster sauce**
- **1 tablespoon soy sauce**
- **1 teaspoon toasted sesame oil**
- **¼ teaspoon ground black pepper**
- **1 bag (8 ounces) coleslaw or broccoli slaw mix**
- **½ red bell pepper, cut into thin strips**
- **½ pound large raw shrimp, peeled, deveined and cut into ¼-inch pieces**
- **3 tablespoons salted dry roasted peanuts, coarsely chopped**
- **¼ cup hoisin sauce**
- **10 to 12 leaves romaine lettuce, rib removed and patted dry**
- **Fresh chives (optional)**

1 Heat peanut oil in large skillet over medium-high heat. Add chicken; cook and stir until browned. Transfer to bowl.

2 Add leeks, mushrooms, celery, water, oyster sauce, soy sauce, sesame oil and black pepper to skillet; cook and stir 5 minutes or until mushrooms are tender. Add slaw and bell pepper; cook and stir until slaw is wilted and bell pepper is softened. Return chicken to skillet; cook and stir until cooked through.

3 Add shrimp to skillet; cook and stir until pink and opaque. Remove from heat; stir in peanuts.

4 Spread about 1 teaspoon hoisin sauce on each lettuce leaf; top with about 2 tablespoons meat mixture. Tightly roll up; tie with chives, if desired.

Crab Rangoon with Spicy Dipping Sauce

makes about 44 wontons

Dipping Sauce

1 cup ketchup

¼ cup chili garlic sauce

4 teaspoons Chinese hot mustard

Crab Rangoon

1 package (8 ounces) cream cheese, softened

1 can (6 ounces) lump crabmeat, well drained

⅓ cup minced green onions

1 package (12 ounces) wonton wrappers

1 egg white, beaten

Vegetable oil for frying

1. Combine ketchup, chili garlic sauce and mustard in small bowl; mix well.
2. Beat cream cheese in medium bowl with electric mixer at medium speed until light and fluffy. Stir in crabmeat and green onions.
3. Working with one at a time, place wonton wrapper on work surface. Place rounded teaspoon crab mixture in center of wrapper. Brush inside edges of wrapper with egg white. Fold wrapper diagonally in half to form triangle; press edges firmly to seal.
4. Heat 2 inches of oil in large saucepan to 350°F over medium-high heat; adjust heat to maintain temperature during frying.
5. Cook wontons in batches 2 minutes per side or until golden brown. Drain on paper towel-lined plate. Serve immediately with dipping sauce.

Baked Crab Rangoon Arrange filled wontons 1 inch apart on parchment-lined baking sheets. Spray tops of triangles with nonstick cooking spray. Bake in preheated 375°F oven 11 minutes or until lightly browned.

Braised Lion's Head

makes 4 servings

Meatballs

- 1 pound ground pork
- 4 ounces raw shrimp, peeled and finely chopped
- ¼ cup sliced water chestnuts, finely chopped
- 1 egg
- 1 green onion, finely chopped
- 1 tablespoon cornstarch
- 1 tablespoon dry sherry
- 1 tablespoon soy sauce
- 1 teaspoon minced fresh ginger
- ½ teaspoon salt
- ½ teaspoon sugar
- 2 tablespoons vegetable oil

Sauce

- 1½ cups chicken broth
- 2 tablespoons soy sauce
- ½ teaspoon sugar
- 1 head napa cabbage, cored and cut into wedges
- 3 tablespoons cold water
- 2 tablespoons cornstarch
- 1 teaspoon toasted sesame oil

1. For meatballs, combine pork, shrimp, water chestnuts, egg, green onion, 1 tablespoon cornstarch, sherry, 1 tablespoon soy sauce, ginger, salt and ½ teaspoon sugar in large bowl; mix well. Shape mixture into eight balls.
2. Heat vegetable oil in wok or large nonstick skillet over medium-high heat. Add meatballs; cook 6 to 8 minutes until browned, turning once.
3. Transfer meatballs to large saucepan; discard drippings. Add broth, 2 tablespoons soy sauce and ½ teaspoon sugar. Bring to a boil. Reduce heat to low; cover and simmer 30 minutes.
4. Place cabbage over meatballs. Cover and cook 10 minutes.
5. Using slotted spoon, transfer meatballs and cabbage to serving platter. Stir 3 tablespoons water into 2 tablespoons cornstarch in small bowl until smooth. Gradually add to pan juices, stirring constantly; cook until slightly thickened. Stir in sesame oil. Serve sauce over meatballs and cabbage.

Pot Stickers

makes about 3 dozen pot stickers

2 cups all-purpose flour, plus additional for work surface

¾ cup plus 2 tablespoons boiling water

½ cup very finely chopped napa cabbage

8 ounces ground pork

2 tablespoons finely chopped water chestnuts

1 green onion, finely chopped

1½ teaspoons cornstarch

1½ teaspoons dry sherry

1½ teaspoons soy sauce

½ teaspoon minced fresh ginger

½ teaspoon toasted sesame oil

¼ teaspoon sugar

2 tablespoons vegetable oil

⅔ cup chicken broth

Soy sauce, vinegar and chili oil

1. Place 2 cups flour in large bowl; make well in center. Pour in boiling water; stir with wooden spoon until dough forms. Knead dough on lightly floured surface about 5 minutes or until smooth and satiny. Cover dough; let rest 30 minutes.

2. For filling, squeeze cabbage to remove as much moisture as possible; place in large bowl. Add pork, water chestnuts, green onion, cornstarch, sherry, soy sauce, ginger, sesame oil and sugar; mix well.

3. Divide dough into two equal portions; cover one portion with plastic wrap or clean towel while working with other portion. Roll out dough to ⅛-inch thickness on lightly floured surface. Cut out 3-inch circles with cookie or biscuit cutter. Place rounded teaspoon filling in center of each dough circle.

4. To shape each pot sticker, lightly moisten edges of one dough circle with water; fold in half. Starting at one end, pinch edges together making four pleats along edge; set dumpling down firmly, seam side up. Cover finished dumplings while shaping remaining dumplings. (Dumplings may be refrigerated for up to 4 hours or freeze on baking sheet and transfer to large resealable food storage bag.)

5. To cook dumplings, heat 1 tablespoon vegetable oil in large nonstick skillet over medium heat. Place half of pot stickers in skillet, seam side up. (Do not thaw frozen dumplings.) Cook 5 to 6 minutes or until bottoms are golden brown.

6 Pour in ⅓ cup broth; cover tightly. Reduce heat to low. Simmer 10 minutes or until all liquid is absorbed (15 minutes if frozen). Repeat with remaining vegetable oil, dumplings and broth. Serve with soy sauce, vinegar and chili oil for dipping.

Veggie Sushi Rolls

makes 24 pieces (about 4 servings)

- **2 tablespoons unseasoned rice vinegar**
- **1 teaspoon sugar**
- **½ teaspoon salt**
- **2 cups cooked short grain brown rice or Sushi Rice (page 145)***
- **4 sheets sushi nori**
- **1 teaspoon toasted sesame seeds**
- **½ English cucumber, cut into ¼-inch thin pieces**
- **½ red bell pepper, cut into ¼-inch thin pieces**
- **½ ripe avocado, cut into ½-inch thin pieces**
- **Pickled ginger and/or wasabi paste (optional)**

If using Sushi Rice, skip step 1.

1. Combine vinegar, sugar and salt in large bowl. Stir in rice. Cover with damp towel until ready to use.
2. Prepare small bowl with water and splash of vinegar to rinse fingers and prevent rice from sticking while working. Place one sheet of nori horizontally on bamboo sushi mat or parchment paper, rough side up. Using wet fingers, spread about ½ cup rice evenly over nori, leaving 1-inch border along bottom edge. Sprinkle rice with ¼ teaspoon sesame seeds. Place one fourth each of cucumber, bell pepper and avocado on top of rice.
3. Pick up edge of mat nearest you. Roll mat forward, wrapping rice around fillings and pressing gently to form log. Press gently to seal. Place roll on cutting board, seam side down. Repeat with remaining nori and fillings.
4. Slice each roll into six pieces using sharp knife.* Cut off ends, if desired. Serve with pickled ginger and/or wasabi, if desired.

**Wipe knife with damp cloth between cuts, if necessary.*

Scallion Pancakes

makes 32 wedges

2 cups all-purpose flour, plus additional for work surface

1 teaspoon sugar

⅔ cup boiling water

¼ to ½ cup cold water

2 teaspoons toasted sesame oil

½ cup finely chopped green onion tops

1 teaspoon coarse salt

½ to ¾ cup vegetable oil

1 Combine 2 cups flour and sugar in large bowl. Stir in boiling water; mix with fork just until water is absorbed and mixture forms large clumps. Gradually stir in enough cold water until dough forms a ball and is no longer sticky.

2 Knead dough on lightly floured surface 5 minutes or until smooth and elastic. Wrap dough with plastic wrap; let stand 1 hour.

3 Knead dough briefly on lightly floured surface; divide into four pieces. Roll one piece into 6- to 7-inch round (keep remaining pieces wrapped in plastic wrap to prevent drying out). Brush dough with ½ teaspoon sesame oil; sprinkle evenly with 2 tablespoons green onions and ¼ teaspoon salt. Roll up dough into tight cylinder.

4 Coil cylinder into a spiral and pinch end under into dough. Repeat with remaining dough pieces, sesame oil, green onions and salt. Cover with plastic wrap and let stand 15 minutes.

5 Roll each piece of dough into 6- to 7-inch round on lightly floured surface with floured rolling pin.

6 Heat ½ cup vegetable oil in wok over medium-high heat to 375°F; adjust heat to maintain temperature during frying. Carefully place one pancake into hot oil. Fry 2 to 3 minutes per side or until golden. While pancake is frying, press center lightly with metal spatula to ensure even cooking. Remove to paper towels to drain. Repeat with remaining pancakes, adding additional oil if necessary.

7 Cut each pancake into eight wedges. Serve immediately.

Vietnamese Vegetarian Spring Rolls

makes 14 rolls

- **1 package (1 ounce) dried mushrooms**
- **1 large carrot, julienned**
- **2 teaspoons sugar, divided**
- **Hoisin Peanut Dipping Sauce (page 19)**
- **3 cups plus 2 tablespoons vegetable oil, divided**
- **1 medium yellow onion, sliced**
- **1 clove garlic, minced**
- **1 tablespoon soy sauce**
- **1 teaspoon sesame oil**
- **1½ cups fresh bean sprouts (4 ounces), rinsed and drained**
- **14 (7-inch) egg roll wrappers**
- **1 egg, beaten**

1. Place mushrooms in bowl; cover with hot water. Let stand 30 minutes. Drain mushrooms, reserving ½ cup liquid. Squeeze out excess water. Cut stems off mushrooms; discard. Thinly slice caps.
2. Combine carrot and 1 teaspoon sugar in medium bowl; let stand 15 minutes, tossing occasionally.
3. Meanwhile, prepare Hoisin Peanut Dipping Sauce; set aside.
4. Heat 2 tablespoons vegetable oil in wok over medium-high. Add onion; stir-fry 1 minute. Stir in mushrooms, garlic and reserved mushroom liquid. Reduce heat to medium; cover and cook 3 minutes or until mushrooms are tender. Add soy sauce, sesame oil and remaining 1 teaspoon sugar; cook and stir 3 to 5 minutes or until all liquid has evaporated. Transfer mixture to medium bowl; cool slightly.
5. Stir carrot and bean sprouts into mushroom mixture. Working with one at a time, place one wrapper on work surface with one corner facing you; keep remaining wrappers covered with plastic wrap. Drain mushroom mixture; place 3 tablespoons mixture on bottom third of wrapper. Brush edges of wrapper with some beaten egg. Fold bottom and sides in over filling; roll up. Place finished rolls on baking sheet; cover with plastic wrap.
6. Heat remaining 3 cups vegetable oil in wok over medium-high heat to 375°F; adjust heat to maintain temperature during frying. Cook rolls in batches 2 to 3 minutes or until golden brown, turning once. Drain on paper towels. Serve with sauce.

Hoisin Peanut Dipping Sauce Combine 2 tablespoons peanut butter, 2 tablespoons water and 1 tablespoon soy sauce in small bowl; stir until smooth. Stir in ⅓ cup hoisin sauce, ½ teaspoon toasted sesame oil, 1 clove garlic, minced, and dash of hot pepper sauce. Makes ½ cup.

Shrimp Ramen Egg Rolls

makes 10 egg rolls

1 tablespoon vegetable oil, plus additional for frying

8 ounces small raw shrimp, peeled, deveined and coarsely chopped

1 cup diced red bell pepper

1 package (3 ounces) shrimp-flavored ramen noodles

2 tablespoons chopped green onion

10 egg roll wrappers

Sweet and sour sauce

1 Heat 1 tablespoon oil in large skillet over medium-high heat. Add shrimp and bell pepper; cook and stir 5 minutes or until shrimp are pink and opaque and bell pepper is softened. Transfer to large bowl.

2 Break noodles into large chunks; set seasoning packet aside. Cook noodles according to package directions; drain and rinse under cold water to stop cooking. Add noodles to bowl with shrimp. Stir in reserved seasoning packet and green onion; mix well.

3 Place one egg roll wrapper on work surface with one corner facing you. Place 2 tablespoons filling across center. Fold bottom and sides in over filling; roll up. Moisten edge with water to seal. Repeat with remaining wrappers and filling.

4 Heat 1 inch oil in large skillet to 350°F. Cook egg rolls in batches about 2 minutes per side or until golden brown. Drain on paper towels. Serve with sweet and sour sauce.

Baked Variation Preheat oven to 375°F. Place egg rolls on baking sheet; brush tops of egg rolls with vegetable oil. Bake 15 minutes or until crisp.

Beer Batter Tempura

makes 4 servings

Dipping Sauce

- **½ cup soy sauce**
- **2 tablespoons rice wine**
- **1 tablespoon sugar**
- **½ teaspoon white vinegar**
- **2 teaspoons minced fresh ginger**
- **1 clove garlic, minced**
- **2 green onions, thinly sliced**

Tempura

- **1½ cups all-purpose flour**
- **1½ cups Japanese beer, chilled**
- **1 teaspoon salt**
- **Vegetable oil for frying**
- **½ pound green beans or asparagus tips**
- **1 large sweet potato, cut into ¼-inch slices**
- **1 medium eggplant or large zucchini, cut into ¼-inch slices**

1. For dipping sauce, combine soy sauce, rice wine, sugar and vinegar in small saucepan; cook and stir over medium heat 3 minutes or until sugar dissolves. Add ginger and garlic; cook and stir 2 minutes. Stir in green onions; remove from heat.

2. For tempura, combine flour, beer and salt in medium bowl just until mixed. Batter should be thin and lumpy. *Do not overmix.* Let stand 15 minutes.

3. Heat 3 inches of oil in large saucepan over medium-high heat to 375°F; adjust heat to maintain temperature during frying.

4. Dip 10 to 12 green beans in batter; add to hot oil. Fry until light golden brown. Drain vegetables on paper towel-lined wire racks. Repeat with sweet potato, then eggplant; do not crowd vegetables during frying. Serve with sauce.

Okonomiyaki (Savory Pancake)

makes 4 servings

- **2 eggs**
- **1 cup all-purpose flour**
- **½ teaspoon salt**
- **1 cup finely chopped cabbage**
- **2 green onions, chopped**
- **¾ to 1 cup water**
- **4 teaspoons vegetable oil**
- **1⅓ cups assorted fillings: cooked chicken or beef, cubed tofu, sliced red bell pepper, asparagus, corn and/or mushrooms**

Sauce

- **¼ cup ketchup**
- **1½ tablespoons Worcestershire sauce**
- **2 tablespoons sake**
- **1 teaspoon tamari or soy sauce**
- **¼ teaspoon Dijon mustard**
- **Mayonnaise (optional)**

1 Whisk eggs in medium bowl. Whisk in flour and salt in medium bowl until combined. (Some lumps are fine.) Stir in cabbage, green onions and ¾ cup water. Add enough additional water to make batter the consistency of thick pancake batter.

2 Heat large nonstick skillet or griddle over medium-high heat. Brush skillet with 1 teaspoon oil; ladle in one fourth of batter and spread into circle. Cook 2 minutes; arrange fillings on top and press gently into batter with spatula. Cook 2 to 3 minutes until edges of pancake look dull and underside is lightly browned. Turn pancake and continue cooking 2 to 4 minutes or until cooked through. Keep warm; repeat with remaining oil, batter and fillings.

3 Meanwhile for sauce, combine ketchup, Worcestershire sauce, sake, tamari and mustard in small saucepan. Simmer over medium-low heat 1 minute, stirring constantly. Let cool to room temperature.

4 Drizzle okonomiyaki with sauce and serve with mayonnaise, if desired.

Fried Tofu with Sesame Dipping Sauce

makes 4 servings

- **3 tablespoons soy sauce**
- **2 tablespoons unseasoned rice vinegar**
- **2 teaspoons sugar**
- **1 teaspoon sesame seeds, toasted***
- **1 teaspoon toasted sesame oil**
- **⅛ teaspoon red pepper flakes**
- **1 package (about 14 ounces) extra firm tofu**
- **¼ cup all-purpose flour or cornstarch**
- **1 egg**
- **¾ cup panko bread crumbs**
- **4 tablespoons vegetable oil**

To toast sesame seeds, spread seeds in small skillet. Shake skillet over medium-low heat about 3 minutes or until seeds begin to pop and turn golden.

1. Whisk soy sauce, vinegar, sugar, sesame seeds, sesame oil and red pepper flakes in small bowl until well blended; set aside.
2. Drain tofu and press between paper towels to remove excess water. Cut crosswise into four slices; cut each slice diagonally into triangles. Place flour in shallow dish. Beat egg in shallow bowl. Place panko in another shallow bowl.
3. Dip each piece of tofu in flour, turning to lightly coat all sides. Dip in egg, letting excess drip back into bowl. Roll in panko to coat.
4. Heat 2 tablespoons vegetable oil in large nonstick skillet over high heat. Reduce heat to medium; add half of tofu in single layer. Cook 1 to 2 minutes per side or until golden brown. Repeat with remaining tofu. Serve with sauce for dipping.

Papaya-Pineapple Smoothie

makes 2 servings (16 ounces)

- **½ (20-ounce) can pineapple chunks in juice**
- **2 cups fresh papaya chunks**
- **1 tablespoon lime juice**
- **1 to 2 tablespoons powdered sugar***
- **Lime wedges and papaya cubes (optional)**

****Increase powdered sugar to 2 tablespoons, depending on sweetness of papaya.***

1. Drain pineapple; measure ½ cup juice. Place pineapple chunks in freezer 30 minutes or until frozen. Refrigerate juice until ready to use.
2. Place papaya and frozen pineapple chunks in blender. Add reserved pineapple juice, lime juice and powdered sugar; process until smooth.
3. Pour into glasses. Garnish with lime wedges and papaya cubes.

Berry Smoothie

makes 1 serving (10 ounces)

1½ cups ice cubes
½ banana
½ cup fresh raspberries
½ cup sliced fresh strawberries
½ cup fresh blueberries
½ cup packed torn spinach

Combine ice, banana, raspberries, strawberries, blueberries and spinach in blender; blend until smooth. Pour into glass.

Note Fresh or frozen berries can be used to make this recipe. When using frozen fruit, reduce the amount of ice used.

Tropical Green Smoothie

makes 2 servings (16 ounces)

- 1 cup ice cubes
- 1 cup packed stemmed kale
- 1 cup frozen tropical fruit mix*
- ½ cup orange juice
- 2 tablespoons honey or agave nectar

**Tropical fruit mix typically contains pineapple, mango and strawberries along with other fruit.*

1. Combine ice, kale, tropical fruit mix, orange juice and honey in blender; blend until smooth.
2. Pour into two glasses.

Strawberry-Banana Smoothie

makes 2 servings (16 ounces)

1½ cups ice cubes
½ banana
½ cup fresh strawberries, hulled
½ cup orange juice
¼ avocado

1. Combine ice, banana, strawberries, orange juice and avocado in blender; blend until smooth.
2. Pour into two glasses.

Peaches & Green Smoothie

makes 1 serving (about 12 ounces)

1 cup loosely packed spinach
1 cup frozen sliced peaches
1 cup ice cubes
¾ cup almond milk
1 tablespoon honey
⅛ teaspoon vanilla

Combine spinach, peaches, ice, almond milk, honey and vanilla in blender; blend until smooth.

Almond Milk Tea with Tapioca

makes 2 servings (20 ounces)

- **3½ cups water**
- **2 black tea bags**
- **4 teaspoons sugar**
- **¼ teaspoon almond extract**
- **1 tablespoon quick-cooking tapioca**
- **4 tablespoons whole milk**
- **Ice cubes**

1. Bring water to a boil in medium saucepan over medium-high heat. Pour 2 cups boiling water over tea bags in teapot. Steep tea 4 minutes or until very dark. Remove and discard tea bags. Stir in sugar and almond extract; cool to room temperature.
2. Meanwhile, add tapioca to remaining 1½ cups boiling water. Boil over medium-high heat 3 to 4 minutes or until tapioca is translucent and cooked through. Drain tapioca in fine-mesh strainer; rinse under cold water until cool.
3. Divide tapioca between two tall glasses; pour 2 tablespoons milk into each glass. Fill each glass three-fourths full with ice. Divide tea between glasses; stir to combine. Serve immediately.

Mango Yogurt Drink

makes 1 serving (12 ounces)

- **½ cup plain yogurt**
- **1 ripe mango, peeled, seeded and sliced**
- **¼ cup orange juice**
- **1 teaspoon honey**
- **2 ice cubes**
- **Milk (optional)**

1. Combine yogurt, mango, orange juice, honey and ice in blender; blend until smooth.
2. Add enough milk to thin to desired consistency. Pour into glass.

Pear-Avocado Smoothie

makes 2 servings (16 ounces)

- **1½ cups ice cubes**
- **1 pear, peeled and cubed**
- **1 cup apple juice**
- **½ avocado**
- **½ cup fresh mint**
- **2 tablespoons fresh lime juice**

1. Combine ice, pear, apple juice, avocado, mint and lime juice in blender; blend until smooth.
2. Pour into two glasses.

Soups & Salads

Egg Drop Soup

makes 4 servings

- 2 cans (about 14 ounces each) vegetable or chicken broth
- 1 tablespoon soy sauce
- 2 teaspoons cornstarch
- 2 eggs, beaten
- ¼ cup thinly sliced green onions

1. Bring broth to a boil in large saucepan over high heat. Reduce heat to medium-low.
2. Stir soy sauce and cornstarch in small bowl until smooth and well blended; stir into broth. Cook and stir 2 minutes or until slightly thickened. Stirring constantly in one direction, slowly pour in eggs in thin stream.
3. Ladle soup into bowls; sprinkle with green onions.

Orange-Ginger Ramen Slaw

makes 6 to 8 servings

- **1 package (3 ounces) ramen noodles, coarsely crumbled***
- **1 tablespoon sesame seeds**
- **6 cups finely shredded green cabbage**
- **2 cups shredded carrots**
- **½ cup diced red onion**
- **½ cup raisins**
- **¾ cup orange marmalade**
- **¼ cup cider vinegar**
- **¼ cup vegetable or canola oil**
- **3 tablespoons grated fresh ginger**
- **1 tablespoon soy sauce**
- **1 teaspoon grated orange peel (optional)**
- **1 teaspoon hot pepper sauce *or* ¼ teaspoon red pepper flakes**
- **¼ teaspoon salt**

Use any flavor; discard seasoning packet.

1 Heat medium skillet over medium-high heat. Add noodles and sesame seeds; cook 2 minutes or until lightly browned, stirring frequently. Transfer to plate.

2 Combine cabbage, carrots, onion and raisins in large bowl. Whisk marmalade, vinegar, oil, ginger, soy sauce, orange peel, if desired, hot pepper sauce and salt in medium bowl until well blended. Add to cabbage mixture; mix well. Cover and refrigerate at least 20 minutes.

3 Sprinkle with noodles and sesame noodles before serving.

Japanese Noodle Soup

makes 6 servings

- **1 package (8½ ounces) Japanese udon noodles**
- **1 tablespoon vegetable oil**
- **1 red bell pepper, cut into thin strips**
- **1 carrot, diagonally sliced**
- **2 green onions, thinly sliced**
- **2 cans (about 14 ounces each) vegetable or beef broth**
- **1 cup water**
- **1 tablespoon soy sauce**
- **½ teaspoon grated fresh ginger**
- **½ teaspoon black pepper**
- **2 cups thinly sliced stemmed shiitake mushrooms**
- **4 ounces daikon (Japanese radish), peeled and cut into thin strips**
- **4 ounces firm tofu, drained and cut into ½-inch cubes**

1. Cook noodles according to package directions. Drain and rinse noodles; set aside.
2. Heat oil in large saucepan over medium-high heat. Add bell pepper, carrot and green onions; cook and stir about 3 minutes or until vegetables are slightly softened. Stir in broth, water, soy sauce, ginger and black pepper; bring to a boil. Stir in mushrooms, daikon and tofu. Reduce heat to low; cook 5 minutes.
3. Place noodles in serving bowls; ladle soup over noodles.

Crunchy Thai Salad

makes 6 to 8 servings

Cilantro-Lime Dressing

- 1 cup loosely packed fresh cilantro leaves
- ½ cup vegetable oil
- ¼ cup chopped red bell pepper
- 2 tablespoons honey
- 2 tablespoons white vinegar
- 2 tablespoons lime juice
- 2 teaspoons Dijon mustard
- 2 teaspoons minced fresh ginger
- 1 teaspoon toasted sesame oil
- 1 teaspoon salt
- ¼ teaspoon black pepper

Thai Peanut Dressing

- ¼ cup creamy peanut butter
- 2 tablespoons hot water
- 2 tablespoons seasoned rice vinegar
- 2 tablespoons vegetable oil
- 2 tablespoons honey
- 2 tablespoons packed brown sugar
- 4 teaspoons soy sauce
- 1½ teaspoons salt
- ¼ teaspoon ground red pepper

Salad

- Vegetable oil for frying
- 2 bundles cellophane (bean thread) noodles (about 2 ounces)
- ½ (12-ounce) package wonton wrappers, cut into ½-inch strips
- 1 small head napa cabbage, cored and cut into ¼-inch strips
- 1 small head red cabbage, cut into wedges, cored and cut into ¼-inch strips
- 1 cup shredded carrots
- 1 bunch green onions, thinly sliced
- 1 seedless cucumber, peeled and julienned
- 2 cups shelled edamame (thawed if frozen)
- 1½ cups dry roasted peanuts
- ½ cup chopped fresh cilantro
- 2 cups chopped cooked chicken
- 2 avocados, diced

1. For cilantro dressing, combine 1 cup cilantro, ½ cup vegetable oil, bell pepper, 2 tablespoons honey, vinegar, lime juice, mustard, ginger, sesame oil, 1 teaspoon salt and black pepper in blender; blend until smooth.

2. For peanut dressing, whisk peanut butter, hot water, rice vinegar, 2 tablespoons vegetable oil, 2 tablespoons honey, brown sugar, 4 teaspoons soy sauce, 1½ teaspoons salt and ground red pepper in small bowl until well blended.

3. Heat 2 inches of oil in large saucepan over medium-high heat to 375°F. Fry cellophane noodles 5 seconds or until puffed, turning once. Drain on paper towel-lined plate. Use same oil to fry wonton strips in batches 1 to 2 minutes or until lightly browned, stirring occasionally to brown all sides. Drain on paper towel-lined plate.

4 Combine cabbages, carrots, green onions, cucumber, edamame, peanuts and ½ cup chopped cilantro in large bowl. Add cilantro dressing; toss to coat. Add chicken and avocado; stir gently to coat. Divide salad among serving plates; top with fried cellophane noodles and fried wontons; drizzle with peanut dressing.

Chinese Side Salad

makes 4 servings

- **¼ cup peanut or vegetable oil**
- **¼ cup rice wine vinegar**
- **2 tablespoons packed brown sugar**
- **1 cucumber, halved lengthwise and sliced**
- **6 cups torn romaine or leaf lettuce**
- **1 cup chow mein noodles**
- **¼ cup peanuts or coarsely chopped cashew nuts (optional)**

1. Combine oil, vinegar and brown sugar in large bowl; whisk until sugar dissolves. Add cucumbers.* Cover and marinate in refrigerator up to 4 hours.

2. Add lettuce, noodles and peanuts, if desired, to cucumbers; mix well.

At this point, salad may be served immediately.

Asian Noodle Soup

makes 4 servings

- **4 ounces uncooked dried Chinese egg noodles or udon noodles**
- **3 cans (about 14 ounces each) vegetable broth**
- **2 slices fresh ginger**
- **2 cloves garlic, cut into halves**
- **½ cup fresh snow peas, cut into 1-inch pieces**
- **3 tablespoons chopped green onions**
- **1 tablespoon chopped fresh cilantro**
- **1½ teaspoons hot chili oil**
- **½ teaspoon toasted sesame oil**

1. Cook noodles according to package directions. Drain and set aside.
2. Combine broth, ginger and garlic in large saucepan; bring to a boil over high heat. Reduce heat to low; simmer 15 minutes. Remove and discard ginger and garlic.
3. Add snow peas, green onions, cilantro, chili oil and sesame oil to broth; simmer 3 to 5 minutes. Stir in noodles; heat through.

Hot & Sour Soup with Bok Choy

makes 4 servings

- 1 tablespoon toasted sesame oil
- 4 ounces shiitake mushrooms, stems finely chopped and caps thinly sliced
- 2 cloves garlic, minced
- 2 cups mushroom or vegetable broth
- 1 cup plus 2 tablespoons cold water, divided
- 2 tablespoons soy sauce
- 1½ tablespoons rice vinegar or white wine vinegar
- ¼ teaspoon red pepper flakes
- 1½ tablespoons cornstarch
- 2 cups coarsely chopped bok choy leaves or napa cabbage
- 1 package (about 12 ounces) silken extra firm tofu, well drained, cut into ½-inch cubes
- 1 green onion, thinly sliced

1. Heat oil in large saucepan over medium heat. Add mushrooms and garlic; cook and stir 3 minutes. Add broth, 1 cup water, soy sauce, vinegar and red pepper flakes; bring to a boil. Reduce heat to medium; simmer 5 minutes.
2. Stir remaining 2 tablespoons water into cornstarch in small bowl until smooth. Stir into soup; cook 2 minutes or until thickened.
3. Stir in bok choy; cook 2 to 3 minutes or until wilted. Stir in tofu; cook until heated through. Sprinkle with green onion.

Gado-Gado (Indonesian Vegetable Salad)

makes 4 servings

- **8 small red potatoes (1¼ pounds), unpeeled**
- **2 large carrots, peeled**
- **4 ounces fresh green beans, trimmed**
- **1 tablespoon soy sauce**
- **2 teaspoons sugar**
- **8 ounces firm tofu**
- **4 cups water**
- **8 ounces green cabbage, cut into ½-inch-thick slices**
- **4 ounces fresh bean sprouts, rinsed and drained**
- **1 cucumber, peeled and cut crosswise into slices**
- **Tangy Peanut Sauce (page 49)**
- **⅓ cup vegetable oil**
- **4 hard-cooked eggs**

***Cut tofu in half horizontally and place it between layers of paper towels. Place a weighted cutting board on top; let stand 15 to 30 minutes.**

1. Place 12-inch bamboo steamer in wok. Add water to ½ inch below steamer. (Water should not touch steamer.) Remove steamer. Cover wok; bring water to a boil over high heat. Place potatoes in steamer. Place steamer in wok over boiling water. Cover and steam potatoes 10 minutes. Add carrots to potatoes; cover and steam 5 minutes. Add green beans to vegetables in steamer; cover and steam 5 to 10 minutes or until vegetables are fork-tender. Remove steamer from wok; cool vegetables completely. Refrigerate until ready to serve.
2. Combine soy sauce and sugar in small bowl. Place tofu in shallow dish; drizzle with soy sauce mixture. Marinate at room temperature 30 minutes, turning occasionally.
3. Place 4 cups water in wok; bring to a boil over high heat. Add cabbage to wok; cook about 1 minute or just until wilted. Remove with slotted spoon to bowl of cold water. Add sprouts to boiling water in wok. Cook 10 seconds and drain in colander. Rinse sprouts under cold water and place in small bowl. Drain cabbage in colander. Refrigerate bean sprouts and cabbage.
4. Prepare Tangy Peanut Sauce.
5. Heat oil in wok over high heat. Add tofu; cook about 5 minutes per side or until well browned, carefully turning once. Drain on paper towels. Cut tofu into ¾-inch squares.
6. Cut cooked beans into 2-inch lengths. Cut carrots into julienne strips. Cut potatoes into ½-inch-thick slices. Cut eggs into wedges.

7 Divide cabbage, carrots and beans among serving plates. Arrange potatoes, eggs and cucumber on top. Top with tofu squares, sprouts and sauce.

Tangy Peanut Sauce

makes about 1 cup

- **1 tablespoon vegetable oil**
- **3 shallots *or* ½ small yellow onion, finely chopped**
- **2 cloves garlic, minced**
- **1 tablespoon packed brown sugar**
- **½ teaspoon salt**
- **¼ to ½ teaspoon ground red pepper**
- **½ cup creamy peanut butter**
- **½ to ⅔ cup water, divided**
- **2 to 3 tablespoons lime juice**

1 Heat oil in small saucepan over medium heat. Add shallots and garlic; cook and stir 1 minute. Stir in brown sugar, salt and ground red pepper to taste. Remove from heat.

2 Stir in peanut butter and ½ cup water until smooth. Stir in lime juice to taste. If sauce is thick, stir in more water, 1 tablespoon at a time, until desired consistency is reached.

Marinated Cucumbers

makes 4 to 6 servings

- **1 large cucumber**
- **2 tablespoons rice vinegar**
- **2 tablespoons peanut or vegetable oil**
- **2 tablespoons soy sauce**
- **1½ teaspoons sugar**
- **1 clove garlic, minced**
- **¼ teaspoon red pepper flakes**

1. Score cucumber lengthwise with tines of fork. Cut in half lengthwise; scrape out and discard seeds. Cut crosswise into ⅛-inch slices; place in medium bowl.

2. Combine vinegar, oil, soy sauce, sugar, garlic and red pepper flakes in small bowl; mix well. Pour dressing over cucumber; toss to coat. Cover and refrigerate at least 4 hours or up to 2 days.

Quick Hot & Sour Chicken Soup

makes 4 servings

- 2 cups water
- 2 cups chicken broth
- 1 package (about 10 ounces) refrigerated fully cooked chicken breast strips, cut into bite-size pieces
- 1 package (about 7 ounces) chicken-flavored rice and vermicelli mix
- 1 jalapeño pepper, minced
- 2 green onions, chopped
- 1 tablespoon soy sauce
- 1 tablespoon lime juice
- 1 tablespoon minced fresh cilantro

1. Combine water, broth, chicken, rice mix, jalapeño, green onions and soy sauce in large saucepan; bring to a boil over high heat. Reduce heat to low. Cover and simmer 20 minutes or until rice is tender, stirring occasionally.
2. Stir in lime juice and sprinkle with cilantro.

Orange-Ramen Tossed Salad

makes 4 servings

- ⅓ cup olive oil
- 2 tablespoons cider vinegar
- 2 teaspoons honey
- 2 teaspoons dried tarragon
- ½ teaspoon dry mustard
- ¼ teaspoon salt
- ⅛ teaspoon black pepper
- 1 can (11 ounces) mandarin oranges, drained and 1 tablespoon juice reserved
- 4 cups chopped romaine lettuce
- 1 package (3 ounces) ramen noodles, lightly crumbled*
- ½ cup toasted** pecans, coarsely chopped
- ¼ cup chopped red onion

**Use any flavor; discard seasoning packet.*

***To toast pecans, spread in single layer in small heavy skillet. Cook over medium heat 1 to 2 minutes or until nuts are lightly browned, stirring frequently. Remove from skillet; cool before using.*

1 Whisk oil, vinegar, honey, tarragon, mustard, salt, pepper and reserved mandarin orange juice in large bowl.

2 Add lettuce, oranges, crumbled noodles, pecans and onion to dressing; toss to combine.

Chicken & Meat

Beef & Broccoli

makes 4 servings

- **1 pound beef tenderloin steaks**
- **2 teaspoons minced fresh ginger**
- **2 cloves garlic, minced**
- **1 tablespoon vegetable oil**
- **3 cups broccoli florets**
- **¼ cup water**
- **2 tablespoons teriyaki sauce**
- **3 cups hot cooked rice***

****Prepare 1 cup rice according to package directions to yield about 3 cups cooked rice.***

1. Cut beef crosswise into ⅛-inch-thick slices. Toss beef with ginger and garlic in medium bowl.
2. Heat oil in wok or large nonstick skillet over medium heat. Add half of beef mixture; stir-fry 2 to 3 minutes or until beef is barely pink in center. Remove to medium bowl. Repeat with remaining beef.
3. Add broccoli and water to wok; cover and steam 3 to 5 minutes or until broccoli is crisp-tender.
4. Return beef and any accumulated juices to wok. Add teriyaki sauce; cook and stir until heated through. Serve over rice.

Kung Pao Chicken

makes 4 servings

- 5 teaspoons dry sherry, divided
- 5 teaspoons soy sauce, divided
- 3½ teaspoons cornstarch, divided
- ¼ teaspoon salt
- 2 boneless skinless chicken breasts (about 1½ to 2 pounds), cut into bite-size pieces
- 2 tablespoons chicken broth or water
- 1 tablespoon red wine vinegar
- 1½ teaspoons sugar
- 3 tablespoons vegetable oil, divided
- ⅓ cup cashews
- 6 to 8 small dried red chiles
- 1 cup red and/or green bell pepper pieces
- 1½ teaspoons minced fresh ginger
- 2 green onions, cut into 1½-inch pieces
- 3 cups hot cooked rice*

**Prepare 1 cup rice according to package directions to yield about 3 cups cooked rice.*

1. For marinade, combine 2 teaspoons sherry, 2 teaspoons soy sauce, 2 teaspoons cornstarch and salt in large bowl. Add chicken; stir to coat. Let stand 30 minutes.

2. Combine remaining 3 teaspoons sherry, 3 teaspoons soy sauce, 1½ teaspoons cornstarch, broth, vinegar and sugar in small bowl.

3. Heat 1 tablespoon oil in wok or large skillet over medium heat. Add cashews; stir-fry until lightly toasted. Remove and set aside. Heat remaining 2 tablespoons oil in wok over medium heat. Add chiles; stir-fry 1 minute or until chiles just begin to char.

4. Increase heat to high. Add chicken mixture and bell peppers; stir-fry 2 minutes. Add ginger; stir-fry 1 minute or until chicken is cooked through. Stir in peanuts and green onions. Stir cornstarch mixture; add to wok. Cook and stir until sauce boils and thickens. Serve over rice.

Asian Chicken Meatballs with Spicy Cucumber Salad

makes 6 servings

Sauce

- ¼ cup hoisin sauce
- 3 tablespoons unseasoned rice vinegar
- 1 tablespoon soy sauce
- 1 teaspoon fresh grated ginger
- 2 cloves garlic, minced

Cucumber Salad

- ¼ cup unseasoned rice vinegar
- 2 teaspoons sugar
- 6 mini cucumbers, thinly sliced
- ½ red onion, thinly sliced
- ½ jalapeño pepper, seeded and finely chopped
- 2 tablespoons chopped fresh cilantro

Meatballs

- ½ cup uncooked quinoa
- 1 cup water
- 1 pound ground chicken
- ½ cup panko bread crumbs
- 1 egg
- 1 teaspoon fresh grated ginger
- 1 teaspoon toasted sesame oil
- ¼ cup thinly sliced green onions
- 2 cloves garlic, minced
- ½ teaspoon salt
- 1 tablespoon toasted sesame seeds

1. For sauce, whisk hoisin sauce, 3 tablespoons vinegar, soy sauce, 1 teaspoon ginger and 2 cloves garlic in medium bowl.
2. For cucumber salad, whisk ¼ cup vinegar and sugar in medium bowl. Add cucumbers, onion, jalapeno and cilantro. Combine cucumber salad ingredients in medium bowl; set aside.
3. Preheat oven to 400°F. Line two baking sheets with parchment paper. Place quinoa in fine-mesh strainer; rinse well under cold water. Combine quinoa and 1 cup water in medium saucepan; bring to a boil. Reduce heat to low; cover and simmer 10 to 15 minutes or until quinoa is tender and water is absorbed. Place in large bowl; cool slightly.
4. Add chicken, panko, egg, 1 teaspoon ginger, sesame oil, green onions, 2 cloves garlic and salt to quinoa; mix well. Shape mixture 24 (2-inch) balls. Place on prepared baking sheets.
5. Bake 10 minutes. Brush with some of sauce; bake 3 minutes or until cooked through (165°F). Add meatballs to sauce; stir to coat.
6. Sprinkle meatballs with sesame seeds. Serve with cucumber salad.

Pepper Beef

makes 4 servings

1 tablespoon soy sauce

2 cloves garlic, minced

¼ teaspoon red pepper flakes

1 pound boneless beef top sirloin steak, tenderloin or rib eye steaks

2 packages (3 ounces each) beef-flavored ramen noodles

2 tablespoons peanut or vegetable oil, divided

1 red bell pepper, cut into thin strips

1 yellow or green bell pepper, cut into thin strips

1 small onion, cut into thin strips

¼ cup stir-fry sauce

2 tablespoons rice wine or dry white wine

¼ cup coarsely chopped fresh cilantro

1 Combine soy sauce, garlic and red pepper flakes in medium bowl. Cut beef lengthwise in half, then crosswise into thin slices. Add to sauce; toss to coat.

2 Prepare noodles according to package directions with seasoning packets; drain and keep warm.

3 Heat wok or large skillet over medium-high heat. Add 1 tablespoon oil; heat until hot. Add half of beef mixture; stir-fry 2 to 3 minutes or until beef is barely pink in center. Transfer to bowl. Repeat with remaining beef mixture.

4 Heat remaining 1 tablespoon oil in wok; add bell peppers and onion. Reduce heat to medium; stir-fry 6 to 7 minutes or until vegetables are crisp-tender. Add stir-fry sauce and wine; stir-fry 2 minutes or until heated through.

5 Return beef along with any accumulated juices to wok; stir-fry until heated through. Serve beef over noodles; sprinkle with cilantro.

Sesame Pork with Thai Cucumber Salad

makes 4 servings

1 large or 2 small pork tenderloins (about 1¼ pounds total)

¼ cup soy sauce

2 cloves garlic, minced

Thai Cucumber Salad (recipe follows)

3 tablespoons honey

2 tablespoons brown sugar

1 teaspoon minced fresh ginger

1 to 2 tablespoons toasted sesame seeds*

To toast sesame seeds, spread seeds in small skillet. Shake skillet over medium heat about 1 minute until seeds begin to pop and turn golden.

1 Place pork in large resealable food storage bag. Combine soy sauce and garlic in small cup; pour over pork. Seal bag; turn to coat. Marinate in refrigerator up to 2 hours. Meanwhile prepare Thai Cucumber Salad.

2 Preheat oven to 400°F. Drain pork; reserve 1 tablespoon marinade. Combine honey, brown sugar, ginger and reserved marinade in small bowl.

3 Place pork in shallow foil-lined roasting pan. Brush with half of honey mixture. Roast 10 minutes. Turn pork over; brush with remaining honey mixture; sprinkle with sesame seeds. Roast 10 minutes for small or 15 minutes for large tenderloin or until internal temperature reaches 145°F when tested with meat thermometer inserted into thickest part of pork.

4 Place pork on cutting board; tent with foil; let rest 5 minutes. (Temperature will rise during stand time.) Cut into ½-inch slices and serve with Thai Cucumber Salad.

Thai Cucumber Salad Thinly slice 1 seedless cucumber and ½ red onion; place in medium bowl. Combine ¼ cup unseasoned rice vinegar, 2 tablespoons lime juice and 1 teaspoon sugar in small bowl; stir into vegetables. Cover; refrigerate 30 minutes. Stir in 2 tablespoons chopped fresh cilantro and 2 tablespoons chopped peanuts before serving.

Beef with Snow Peas & Baby Corn

makes 4 servings

1 pound ground beef

1 clove garlic, minced

1 teaspoon vegetable oil

6 ounces snow peas, halved lengthwise

1 red bell pepper, cut into strips

1 can (15 ounces) baby corn, rinsed and drained

1 tablespoon soy sauce

1 teaspoon toasted sesame oil

Salt and black pepper

3 cups hot cooked rice*

Prepare 1 cup rice according to package directions to yield about 3 cups cooked rice.

1 Cook beef and garlic in wok or large skillet 6 to 8 minutes over medium-high heat, stirring to break up meat. Drain fat; remove beef to medium bowl.

2 Heat vegetable oil in wok over medium-high heat. Add snow peas and bell pepper; stir-fry 2 to 3 minutes or until vegetables are crisp-tender.

3 Stir in beef mixture, baby corn, soy sauce and sesame oil; cook until heated through. Season with salt and black pepper. Serve over rice.

Beef Fried Rice

makes 4 servings

- 1 pound ground beef
- 6 green onions, chopped
- 3 stalks celery, chopped
- 8 ounces bean sprouts
- 1 cup sliced mushrooms
- 1 cup finely chopped red bell pepper
- 1 teaspoon grated fresh ginger
- 3 cups cold cooked rice
- 2 tablespoons soy sauce
- Salt and black pepper

1. Brown beef in wok or large skillet over medium-high heat 6 to 8 minutes, stirring to break up meat. Drain fat. Stir in green onions, celery, bean sprouts, mushrooms, bell pepper and ginger; cook and stir 5 minutes or until vegetables are crisp-tender.

2. Stir in rice and soy sauce; stir-fry until heated through. Season with salt and black pepper.

Pork & Vegetable Stir-Fry

makes 4 servings

- ¼ cup water
- 2 teaspoons cornstarch
- 4 tablespoons peanut oil, divided
- 6 whole dried hot red chile peppers
- 4 cloves garlic, sliced
- 1 pork tenderloin (about 12 ounces), thinly sliced
- 1 large carrot, cut into ¼-inch-thick slices*
- 2 ounces oyster, shiitake or button mushrooms, coarsely chopped
- 1 baby eggplant, thinly sliced
- 5 ounces fresh snow peas, ends trimmed
- 3 tablespoons packed brown sugar
- 2 tablespoons fish sauce
- 1 tablespoon toasted sesame oil
- 3 cups hot cooked rice**

**To make scalloped edges on carrot, use citrus stripper or grapefruit spoon to cut groove into carrot, cutting lengthwise from stem end to tip. Continue to cut grooves around carrot about ¼ inch apart. Then cut carrot crosswise into ¼-inch-thick slices.*

***Prepare 1 cup rice according to package directions to yield about 3 cups cooked rice.*

1. Stir water into cornstarch in small bowl until smooth.
2. Heat wok or large skillet 1 minute over high heat. Drizzle 2 tablespoons peanut oil into wok; heat 30 seconds. Add peppers and garlic; stir-fry about 1 minute. Add pork; stir-fry 3 to 4 minutes or until barely pink in center. Remove pork mixture to bowl.
3. Add remaining 2 tablespoons peanut oil to wok. Add carrot, mushrooms and eggplant; stir-fry 2 minutes. Add snow peas and pork mixture; stir-fry 1 minute.
4. Stir cornstarch mixture; add to wok. Cook 1 minute or until sauce thickens. Stir in brown sugar, fish sauce and sesame oil; cook and stir until heated through. Serve over rice.

Teppanyaki

makes 4 servings

- ⅓ cup tamari or soy sauce
- 2 tablespoons mirin (Japanese sweet rice wine)
- 1 tablespoon lemon juice
- 1 tablespoon orange juice
- ⅛ to ¼ teaspoon red pepper flakes (optional)
- 4 frozen ears corn on the cob *or* 8 mini frozen corn on the cob
- 2 to 3 tablespoons vegetable oil
- 2 medium zucchini or yellow squash, cut diagonally into thin slices
- 4 ounces shiitake mushrooms, stemmed and cut into thick slices
- 8 ounces beef tenderloin or top loin steak, thinly sliced crosswise
- 8 ounces pork tenderloin, thinly sliced crosswise
- 8 ounces medium raw shrimp, peeled and deveined

1. For dipping sauce, combine tamari, mirin, lemon juice, orange juice and red pepper flakes, if desired, in small bowl; set aside.
2. Heat oven to 225°F to keep food warm while cooking. Cook corn in microwave according to package directions just until heated through.
3. Heat 1 tablespoon oil in large cast iron or other heavy skillet over medium-high heat. Brown corn about 2 minutes, turning frequently. Place on baking sheet; keep warm in oven.
4. Heat 1 tablespoon oil in same skillet. Add zucchini; cook 2 to 3 minutes or until browned and tender. Place on baking sheet in oven. Add mushrooms to skillet; cook and stir 2 to 3 minutes or until tender. Place on baking sheet in oven.
5. Heat remaining 1 tablespoon oil in same skillet Add beef; cook and stir 2 minutes or until browned and tender. Place on baking sheet in oven. Add pork to skillet; cook and stir about 3 minutes or until cooked through. Place on baking sheet in oven. Add shrimp to skillet; cook and stir 2 to 3 minutes or until pink and opaque.
6. Arrange vegetables and meat on serving plates. Serve with dipping sauce.

Szechuan Grilled Flank Steak

makes 4 to 6 servings

- **1 beef flank steak ($1\frac{1}{4}$ to $1\frac{1}{2}$ pounds)**
- **¼ cup seasoned rice wine vinegar**
- **¼ cup soy sauce**
- **2 tablespoons toasted sesame oil**
- **4 cloves garlic, minced**
- **2 teaspoons minced fresh ginger**
- **½ teaspoon red pepper flakes**
- **¼ cup water**
- **½ cup thinly sliced green onions**
- **2 to 3 teaspoons sesame seeds, toasted**
- **3 cups hot cooked rice***

Prepare 1 cup rice according to package directions to yield about 3 cups cooked rice.

1 Place steak in large resealable food storage bag. Combine vinegar, soy sauce, oil, garlic, ginger and red pepper flakes in small bowl; pour over steak. Seal bag; turn to coat. Marinate in refrigerator 3 hours, turning once.

2 Prepare grill for direct cooking. Remove steak from marinade; pour marinade into small saucepan. Grill steak, uncovered, over medium heat 17 to 21 minutes for medium rare to medium or to desired doneness, turning once.

3 Add water to reserved marinade. Bring to a boil over high heat. Boil 1 minute.

4 Slice steak against the grain into thin slices. Drizzle steak with boiled marinade. Sprinkle with green onions and sesame seeds. Serve with rice, if desired.

Chicken Mushroom Stir-Fry

makes 4 servings

3 tablespoons dry sherry, divided

3 tablespoons soy sauce, divided

1 tablespoon plus 1 teaspoon cornstarch, divided

½ teaspoon toasted sesame oil

1 pound boneless skinless chicken breasts, cut into 1-inch pieces

½ cup chicken broth

2 tablespoons vegetable or peanut oil, divided

1 large onion, coarsely chopped

2 jars (7 ounces each) *or* 1 can (15 ounces) straw mushrooms, drained

2 cloves garlic, minced

Hot cooked Chinese egg noodles or rice (optional)

¼ cup thinly sliced green onions

1 Whisk 1 tablespoon sherry, 1 tablespoon soy sauce, 1 teaspoon cornstarch and sesame oil in large bowl until smooth. Add chicken; toss to coat. Marinate at room temperature 10 minutes.

2 Whisk broth, remaining 2 tablespoons sherry, 2 tablespoons soy sauce and 1 tablespoon cornstarch in small bowl until smooth; set aside.

3 Heat 1 tablespoon vegetable oil in wok or large skillet over medium-high heat. Add chicken mixture; stir-fry 7 minutes or until chicken is cooked through. Remove to plate.

4 Heat remaining 1 tablespoon vegetable oil in wok. Add onion; stir-fry 3 minutes or until crisp-tender. Add mushrooms; stir-fry 3 minutes. Add garlic; stir-fry 30 seconds.

5 Return chicken to wok. Stir cornstarch mixture; add to wok. Cook and stir 2 minutes or until chicken is heated through and sauce thickens. Serve over noodles, if desired. Sprinkle with green onions.

Sweet & Spicy Chicken

makes 4 servings

- **1 cut-up whole chicken (about 3 pounds)**
- **1 tablespoon vegetable oil**
- **Salt and black pepper**
- **½ cup chicken broth**
- **¼ cup soy sauce**
- **2 tablespoons honey**
- **1 tablespoon tomato paste**
- **3 cloves garlic, chopped**
- **2 teaspoons ground ginger**
- **½ teaspoon ground red pepper**
- **¼ cup sliced green onions**

1. Preheat oven to 400°F. Place chicken pieces on rack of roasting pan. Brush chicken with oil; sprinkle with salt and black pepper. Bake 20 minutes.
2. Meanwhile combine broth, soy sauce, honey, tomato paste, garlic, ginger and red pepper in small saucepan over medium-high heat. Cook and stir 10 to 15 minutes or until sauce has thickened. Reserve half of sauce for serving.
3. Remove chicken from oven. *Reduce oven temperature to 350°F.* Baste chicken with remaining sauce. Bake 30 minutes or until chicken is cooked through (165°F); baste with sauce halfway through cooking time. Serve chicken with reserved sauce; garnish with green onions.

Sukiyaki

makes 4 servings

1 package ($3^3/_4$ ounces) cellophane noodles (bean threads)

½ cup beef broth

½ cup teriyaki sauce

¼ cup sake, rice wine or dry sherry

1 tablespoon sugar

1 pound beef tenderloin or top sirloin steaks

2 tablespoons vegetable oil, divided

6 ounces fresh shiitake mushrooms, stems removed and sliced

8 ounces firm tofu, drained and cut into 1-inch cubes

6 green onions, cut into 2-inch pieces

8 ounces fresh spinach, stemmed

1 Place noodles in bowl; cover with water. Let stand 30 minutes or until softened; drain. Cut into 4-inch lengths; set aside.

2 Combine beef broth, teriyaki sauce, sake and sugar in small bowl; mix well. Set aside. Cut beef crosswise into ¼-inch strips.

3 Heat wok over high heat 1 minute. Drizzle 1 tablespoon oil into wok and heat 30 seconds. Add half of beef; stir-fry 3 minutes or until browned. Remove to bowl; set aside. Repeat with remaining 1 tablespoon oil and beef.

4 Reduce heat to medium. Add mushrooms to wok; stir-fry 1 minute and move up one side of wok. Add tofu to bottom of wok; fry 1 minute, stirring gently. Move up another side of wok. Add green onions to bottom of wok. Add broth mixture and bring to a boil. Move onions up side of wok.

5 Add noodles and spinach, keeping each in separate piles and stirring gently to soften in teriyaki sauce. Push up side of wok. Add beef and any juices; heat through.

Japanese Fried Chicken with Watercress Salad

makes 4 servings

1 pound boneless skinless chicken breasts, cut into 2-inch pieces
3 tablespoons tamari or soy sauce
2 tablespoons sake
3 cloves garlic, minced
1 teaspoon minced fresh ginger
Vegetable oil for frying
⅓ cup cornstarch
3 tablespoons all-purpose flour

Salad

¼ cup unseasoned rice vinegar
3 teaspoons tamari or soy sauce
1 teaspoon toasted sesame oil
2 bunches watercress, stemmed
1 pint grape tomatoes, halved

1 Place chicken in resealable food storage bag. Mix 3 tablespoons tamari, sake, garlic and ginger in small bowl; pour over chicken. Seal bag; turn to coat. Marinate in refrigerator at least 30 minutes, turning bag occasionally.

2 Meanwhile, heat 2 inches of oil in large saucepan over medium-high heat to 350°F; adjust heat to maintain temperature during frying. Combine cornstarch and flour in shallow dish. Drain chicken, discarding marinade. Roll chicken pieces in cornstarch mixture and shake off excess.

3 Fry chicken in batches 4 to 6 minutes or until golden and cooked through (165°F). Do not crowd pan. Drain on paper towels.

4 For salad dressing, whisk vinegar, 3 teaspoons tamari and sesame oil in small bowl. Arrange watercress and tomatoes on serving plates. Drizzle with dressing and top with chicken.

Beef with Cashews

makes 4 servings

- 1 boneless beef top sirloin steak (about 1 pound)
- 4 tablespoons vegetable oil, divided
- ½ cup water
- 4 teaspoons cornstarch
- 4 teaspoons soy sauce
- 1 teaspoon toasted sesame oil
- 1 teaspoon oyster sauce
- 1 teaspoon Chinese chili sauce
- 8 green onions with tops, cut into 1-inch pieces
- 1 carrot, julienned or shredded
- 1 piece fresh ginger (about 1-inch square), peeled and minced
- 2 cloves garlic, minced
- ⅔ cup cashews
- Hot cooked rice (optional)
- Chopped chives (optional)

1 Cut beef lengthwise in half, then cut crosswise into ⅛-inch slices.

2 Heat 1 tablespoon vegetable oil in wok or large skillet over high heat. Add half of beef; stir-fry 3 to 5 minutes or until browned. Remove to small bowl. Repeat with 1 tablespoon vegetable oil and remaining beef.

3 Combine water, cornstarch, soy sauce, sesame oil, oyster sauce and chili sauce in small bowl; mix well.

4 Heat remaining 2 tablespoons vegetable oil in wok over high heat. Add green onions, carrot, ginger, garlic and cashews; stir-fry 1 minute. Stir cornstarch mixture; add to wok with beef. Cook and stir until sauce boils and thickens. Serve over rice, if desired; garnish with chives.

Tonkatsu (Breaded Pork Cutlets)

makes 4 servings

Tonkatsu Sauce

¼ cup ketchup
1 tablespoon soy sauce
2 teaspoons sugar
2 teaspoons mirin (Japanese sweet rice wine)
1 teaspoon Worcestershire sauce
½ teaspoon grated fresh ginger
1 clove garlic, minced

Pork

1 pound pork tenderloin, trimmed of fat
½ cup all-purpose flour
Salt and black pepper
2 eggs
2 tablespoons water
1½ cups panko bread crumbs
6 to 8 tablespoons vegetable oil, divided
3 cups hot cooked rice*

****Prepare 1 cup rice according to package directions to yield about 3 cups cooked rice, or prepare Sushi Rice on page 145.***

1 For sauce, combine ketchup, soy sauce, sugar, mirin, Worcestershire sauce, ginger and garlic in small bowl.

2 Slice pork diagonally into ½-inch-thick pieces. Place flour in shallow bowl; season with salt and pepper. Whisk eggs and water in another shallow bowl. Place panko in third shallow bowl. Coat pork in flour mixture. Dip in egg mixture, letting excess drip back into bowl. Coat with panko.

3 Heat 2 tablespoons oil in large nonstick skillet over medium heat. Add pork in single layer; do not crowd pan. Cook 4 minutes per side or until cooked through. Drain on paper towels; keep warm. Repeat with remaining pork, adding additional oil as needed.

4 Serve over rice with sauce.

Donburi (Beef & Rice Bowl)

makes 4 servings

3 teaspoons peanut or vegetable oil, divided

3 eggs, beaten

2 cups broccoli florets

1 yellow onion, cut into thin wedges

1 pound boneless beef top sirloin steak, cut crosswise into thin strips

2 teaspoons cornstarch

¼ cup beef or chicken broth

3 tablespoons tamari or soy sauce

2 teaspoons toasted sesame oil

¼ teaspoon red pepper flakes

¼ cup chopped fresh cilantro

¼ cup chopped green onions

3 cups hot cooked short grain rice*

****Prepare 1 cup rice according to package directions to yield about 3 cups cooked rice, or prepare Sushi Rice on page 145.***

1 Heat 1 teaspoon peanut oil in large nonstick skillet over medium heat. Add eggs; cook 2 minutes without stirring or until bottom of omelet is set. Turn eggs over and cook 1 minute. Slide onto cutting board; let cool. Roll up omelet and cut crosswise into thin slices.

2 Heat 1 teaspoon peanut oil in same skillet. Add broccoli and onion; cook 4 to 5 minutes, stirring occasionally. Transfer to bowl.

3 Combine beef strips and cornstarch in medium bowl. Heat remaining 1 teaspoon peanut oil in same skillet. Add beef; stir-fry 2 minutes. Add broth, tamari, sesame oil and red pepper flakes. Simmer 2 minutes or until sauce thickens.

4 Stir in sliced omelet, reserved vegetables, cilantro and green onions. Stir-fry 1 minute or until heated through. Spoon rice into four shallow bowls; top with beef mixture.

Sweet & Sour Pork

makes 4 servings

- ¼ cup soy sauce
- 1 egg yolk
- 1½ tablespoons dry sherry
- 2 teaspoons sugar
- 2 pounds boneless lean pork, cut into 1-inch pieces
- ½ cup plus 2 tablespoons cornstarch, divided
- 1 can (20 ounces) pineapple chunks in syrup, undrained
- ¼ cup rice vinegar
- 3 tablespoons tomato sauce
- 1 cup water
- 1 cucumber, halved lengthwise, seeded and cut into ¼-inch slices
- 3 cups plus 3 tablespoons vegetable oil, divided
- 1 large yellow onion, thinly sliced
- 8 green onions with tops, diagonally cut into 1-inch pieces
- 1 red or green pepper, chopped
- 4 ounces fresh mushrooms, cut into quarters
- 2 stalks celery, diagonally cut into ½-inch slices

1. For marinade, whisk soy sauce, egg yolk, sherry and sugar in large bowl. Add pork; stir to coat. Cover and refrigerate 1 hour, stirring occasionally.
2. Drain meat, reserving marinade. Place ½ cup cornstarch in large bowl; add pork; toss to coat.
3. Drain pineapple, reserving syrup. Add syrup, vinegar and tomato sauce to reserved marinade. Stir remaining 2 tablespoons cornstarch and water in another small bowl until smooth.
4. Heat 3 cups oil in large skillet over medium-high heat to 375°F. Add half of pork; cook 5 minutes or until no longer pink in center. Drain on paper towel-lined plate. Repeat with remaining pork.
5. Heat remaining 3 tablespoons oil in wok over high heat. Add cucumber, yellow onion, green onions, bell pepper, mushrooms and celery; stir-fry 3 minutes. Stir cornstarch mixture; add to wok with pineapple syrup mixture. Cook and stir until sauce boils and thickens. Add pork and pineapple; stir-fry until heated through.

Fish & Seafood

Asian Baked Cod

makes 4 servings

- 2 tablespoons soy sauce
- 2 tablespoons apple juice
- 1 tablespoon finely chopped fresh ginger
- 2 cloves garlic, minced
- 1 teaspoon crushed Szechuan peppercorns
- 4 cod fillets (about 1 pound)
- 3 cups hot cooked rice*
- 4 green onions, thinly sliced

**Prepare 1 cup rice according to package directions to yield about 3 cups cooked rice.*

1. Preheat oven to 375°F. Spray roasting pan with nonstick cooking spray.
2. Whisk soy sauce, apple juice, ginger, garlic and peppercorns in small bowl until well blended. Place fish in prepared pan; pour soy sauce mixture over fish.
3. Bake 10 minutes or until fish is opaque and flakes easily when tested with fork.
4. Remove fish to serving dish; pour pan juices over fish. Serve with rice; sprinkle with green onions.

Red Snapper with Orange-Plum Sauce

makes 4 servings

- **1 pound red snapper fillets**
- **2 tablespoons soy sauce**
- **½ cup all-purpose flour**
- **¼ teaspoon salt**
- **⅛ teaspoon black pepper**
- **2 to 3 tablespoons plus 1 teaspoon vegetable oil, divided**
- **½ cup orange juice**
- **1 teaspoon cornstarch**
- **1 clove garlic, minced**
- **1 jalapeño pepper, seeded and minced**
- **½ cup plum sauce**
- **2 tablespoons mirin (Japanese rice wine)**
- **1 tablespoon chili garlic sauce**
- **1 tablespoon minced green onion (optional)**

1. Place fish in shallow dish; drizzle with soy sauce and turn to coat. Let stand 30 minutes.
2. Combine flour, salt and black pepper in another shallow bowl. Remove fish from soy sauce; coat with flour mixture.
3. Heat 2 tablespoons oil in large nonstick skillet over medium-high heat. Add fish; shake skillet so fish doesn't stick. (Fillets should not touch in skillet; cook in batches if necessary.) Cook 4 to 5 minutes per side or until fish flakes when tested with fork. Remove fish from skillet; keep warm. If cooking fish in two batches add 1 tablespoon oil to skillet and heat before adding remaining fish.
4. Meanwhile, stir orange juice into cornstarch in small bowl until well blended. Heat remaining 1 teaspoon oil in small saucepan over medium-high heat. Add garlic and jalapeño; cook and stir 1 minute. Add orange juice mixture, plum sauce, mirin and chili garlic sauce; cook and stir 1 minute or until slightly thickened.
5. Arrange fish on plates; top with sauce and garnish with green onion.

Shanghai Fish Packets

makes 4 servings

- **4 tilapia, sole or halibut fillets (6 ounces each)**
- **¼ cup mirin (Japanese rice wine)**
- **3 tablespoons soy sauce**
- **1 tablespoon toasted sesame oil**
- **1½ teaspoons grated fresh ginger**
- **¼ teaspoon red pepper flakes**
- **1 tablespoon peanut or vegetable oil**
- **1 clove garlic, minced**
- **1 package (10 ounces) fresh spinach leaves, stems removed**

1. Prepare grill for direct cooking.
2. Place fish in single layer in large shallow dish. Combine mirin, soy sauce, sesame oil, ginger and red pepper flakes in small bowl; pour over fish. Cover and marinate in refrigerator 20 minutes.
3. Heat peanut oil in large skillet over medium heat. Add garlic; cook and stir 1 minute. Add spinach; cook and stir about 3 minutes until wilted.
4. Place spinach mixture in center of four 12-inch squares of heavy-duty foil. Remove fish from marinade; reserve marinade. Place one fish fillet over each mound of spinach; drizzle with reserved marinade. Wrap in foil to create packet.
5. Grill packets, covered, over medium heat 15 to 18 minutes or until fish begins to flake when tested with fork.

Grilled Swordfish with Hot Red Sauce

makes 4 servings

- **2 tablespoons Sesame Salt (recipe follows)**
- **4 swordfish or halibut steaks (about 1½ pounds total)**
- **¼ cup chopped green onions**
- **2 tablespoons hot bean paste***
- **2 tablespoons soy sauce**
- **4 teaspoons sugar**
- **4 cloves garlic, minced**
- **1 tablespoon toasted sesame oil**
- **⅛ teaspoon black pepper**
- **3 cups hot cooked rice****

Available in specialty stores or Asian markets.

*****Prepare 1 cup rice according to package directions to yield about 3 cups cooked rice.***

1. Prepare Sesame Salt.
2. Rinse fish and pat dry with paper towels. Place in shallow glass dish.
3. Combine green onions, 2 tablespoons Sesame Salt, hot bean paste, soy sauce, sugar, garlic, sesame oil and pepper in small bowl; mix well.
4. Spread mixture over both sides of fish; cover with plastic wrap. Marinate in refrigerator 30 minutes.
5. Prepare grill for direct cooking or preheat broiler. Oil grid or spray broiler rack with nonstick cooking spray.
6. Remove fish from marinade; discard remaining marinade. Grill fish over medium-high heat or broil 4 to 5 minutes per side or until fish is opaque. Serve over rice.

Sesame Salt Heat small skillet over medium heat. Add ¼ cup sesame seeds; cook and stir about 3 minutes or until seeds are golden. Cool. Crush toasted sesame seeds and 1 teaspoon coarse salt with mortar and pestle or process in clean spice grinder. Store in airtight container in refrigerator.

Pan-Cooked Bok Choy Salmon

makes 2 servings

- **1 pound bok choy or napa cabbage, chopped**
- **1 cup broccoli slaw mix**
- **2 tablespoons vegetable oil, divided**
- **2 salmon fillets (4 to 6 ounces each)**
- **¼ teaspoon salt**
- **½ teaspoon black pepper**
- **1 teaspoon sesame seeds**
- **1 tablespoon soy sauce**
- **1 teaspoon toasted sesame oil**

1. Combine bok choy and broccoli slaw mix in colander; rinse and drain well.
2. Heat 1 tablespoon vegetable oil in large skillet over medium heat. Sprinkle salmon with salt and pepper. Add salmon to skillet; cook 3 minutes per side. Remove salmon from skillet.
3. Add remaining 1 tablespoon vegetable oil and sesame seeds to skillet; stir to toast sesame seeds. Add bok choy mixture, soy sauce and sesame oil; cook and stir 3 to 4 minutes.
4. Return salmon to skillet. Reduce heat to low; cover and cook 4 minutes or until salmon begins to flake when tested with fork.

Braised Shrimp with Vegetables

makes 4 servings

½ cup chicken broth
1 teaspoon cornstarch
1 teaspoon oyster sauce
¼ teaspoon sugar
½ teaspoon minced fresh ginger
⅛ teaspoon black pepper
1 tablespoon vegetable oil
1 pound large raw shrimp, peeled and deveined (with tails on)
8 ounces fresh broccoli, coarsely chopped
2 cans (4 ounces each) whole button mushrooms, drained
1 can (8 ounces) sliced bamboo shoots, drained

1. Stir broth into cornstarch in small bowl. Stir in oyster sauce, sugar, ginger and pepper in small bowl; mix well.
2. Heat oil in wok or large skillet over high heat. Add shrimp; stir-fry until shrimp turn pink, about 3 minutes.
3. Add broccoli to wok; stir-fry 1 minute. Add mushrooms and bamboo shoots; stir-fry 1 minute.
4. Stir cornstarch mixture; add to wok. Cook and stir 2 minutes or until sauce boils and thickens.

Crab Cakes Canton

makes 12 cakes

- **7 ounces fresh, frozen or pasteurized crabmeat or imitation crabmeat**
- **1½ cups fresh whole wheat bread crumbs (about 3 slices)**
- **¼ cup thinly sliced green onions**
- **1 clove garlic, minced**
- **1 teaspoon minced fresh ginger**
- **2 egg whites, lightly beaten**
- **1 tablespoon teriyaki sauce**
- **2 tablespoons vegetable oil**
- **Sweet and sour sauce (optional)**

1. Pick out and discard any shell or cartilage from crabmeat. Combine crabmeat, bread crumbs, green onions, garlic and ginger in medium bowl; mix well. Add egg whites and teriyaki sauce; mix well. Shape into patties about ½ inch thick and 2 inches in diameter.*

2. Heat 1 tablespoon oil in large nonstick skillet over medium heat. Add half of crab cakes; cook 2 minutes per side or until golden brown. Remove to serving plate; keep warm. Repeat with remaining 1 tablespoon oil and crab cakes. Serve with sweet and sour sauce, if desired.

**Crab cakes may be made ahead to this point; cover and refrigerate up to 24 hours before cooking.*

Szechuan Tuna Steaks

makes 4 servings

- **4 tuna steaks (6 ounces each), cut 1 inch thick**
- **¼ cup dry sherry or sake**
- **¼ cup soy sauce**
- **1 tablespoon toasted sesame oil**
- **1 teaspoon hot chili oil *or* ¼ teaspoon red pepper flakes**
- **1 clove garlic, minced**
- **3 tablespoons chopped fresh cilantro (optional)**

1. Place tuna in single layer in large shallow dish. Combine sherry, soy sauce, sesame oil, hot chili oil and garlic in small bowl; mix well. Reserve ¼ cup mixture in another small bowl. Pour remaining soy sauce mixture over fish; cover and marinate in refrigerator 40 minutes, turning once.
2. Spray grid with nonstick cooking spray. Prepare grill for direct cooking. Drain fish, discarding marinade.
3. Grill fish, uncovered, over medium-high heat 6 minutes or until tuna is seared but still feels somewhat soft in center,* turning once. Remove to cutting board. Cut into thin slices; drizzle with reserved soy sauce mixture. Garnish with cilantro.

**Tuna becomes dry and tough if overcooked. Cook to medium doneness for best results.*

Sesame Salmon & Rice

makes 4 servings

- **4 salmon fillets (6 ounces each)**
- **1½ cups toasted sesame marinade,* divided**
- **2 cups water**
- **1 cup uncooked rice**
- **1 tablespoon oil**

Toasted sesame marinade can be found in the Asian section of most supermarkets and in Asian specialty markets.

1. Place salmon in shallow dish. Pour 1 cup marinade evenly over fish; gently turn to coat evenly. Marinate in refrigerator 20 minutes.
2. Preheat oven to 400°F. Line baking sheet with foil; spray with nonstick cooking spray.
3. Place salmon, skin side down, on prepared baking sheet; discard marinade. Bake 20 minutes or until just opaque in center.
4. Meanwhile, combine 2 cups water, rice and oil in large saucepan. Bring to a boil. Reduce heat; cover and simmer 15 minutes until water is absorbed. Remove from heat. Cover and let stand 5 minutes.
5. Stir remaining ½ cup marinade into rice. Serve salmon over rice.

Vegetarian Dishes

Asian Stir-Fried Vegetables

makes 4 servings

- **2 tablespoons vegetable oil**
- **1 pound broccoli, asparagus spears, green beans or sliced zucchini or a combination, cut into bite-size pieces**
- **2 cups sliced carrots**
- **1 onion, thinly sliced**
- **1 cup sliced mushrooms**
- **2 tablespoons soy sauce**
- **2 cloves garlic, minced**
- **Salt and black pepper**

1. Heat oil in wok or large skillet over high heat. Add broccoli, carrots, onion and mushrooms; stir-fry 5 minutes or until crisp-tender.
2. Add soy sauce and garlic; cook and stir 1 minute or until garlic is fragrant but not browned. Season to taste with salt and black pepper.

Sesame Ginger Tofu Bahn Mi

makes 4 servings

4 ounces peeled daikon radish *or* 5 medium red radishes
1 large carrot
¾ cup unseasoned rice vinegar
1 tablespoon granulated sugar
1 teaspoon salt
¼ cup soy sauce
1 tablespoon packed brown sugar
1 tablespoon toasted sesame oil
2 teaspoons grated fresh ginger
1 clove garlic, minced
1 package (about 14 ounces) extra firm tofu, drained, pressed and halved crosswise
1 tablespoon vegetable oil
8 ounces seedless cucumber (about 8 inches)
4 French bread sandwich rolls
¼ cup mayonnaise
Fresh cilantro sprigs
1 jalapeño pepper, sliced into rings

1 Spiral radish and carrot with fine spiral blade of spiralizer.* Combine vinegar, granulated sugar and salt in medium bowl; stir to dissolve sugar. Measure 1 cup total of carrot and radish; add to vinegar. Let stand at least 1 hour for flavors to blend.

2 Whisk soy sauce, brown sugar, sesame oil, ginger and garlic in small bowl until smooth. Place tofu in 8-inch square baking dish; pour soy sauce mixture over tofu. Marinate at room temperature 30 minutes to 1 hour, turning occasionally.

3 Drain tofu, discarding marinade. Heat vegetable oil in large cast iron skillet over high heat. Working in batches, cook tofu 3 to 4 minutes per side or until well browned. Transfer to paper towel-lined plate; let stand until cool enough to handle. Cut into thin slices.

4 Spiral cucumber with large spiral blade of spiralizer.* Scoop out some of soft insides of bread. Spread mayonnaise over bottom half of bread; top with tofu, cilantro, cucumber, carrot mixture and jalapeños.

**If you don't have a spiralizer, use a julienne peeler to cut the vegetables or cut into julienne strips with sharp knife.*

Thai Rama with Tofu

makes 4 servings

- **2 heads broccoli (about 1½ pounds), cut into florets**
- **1 package (about 14 ounces) firm or extra firm tofu, drained**
- **Salt and black pepper**
- **½ cup plus 1 tablespoon cornstarch, divided**
- **3 tablespoons plus 2 teaspoons vegetable oil, divided**
- **½ cup finely chopped onion**
- **3 cloves garlic, minced**
- **½ cup peanut butter**
- **3 tablespoons packed brown sugar**
- **2 tablespoons soy sauce**
- **1 teaspoon paprika**
- **¼ teaspoon ground red pepper**
- **1 cup unsweetened coconut milk**
- **1 tablespoon water, plus more if needed**
- **2 tablespoons lime juice**
- **3 cups hot cooked rice***
- **Chopped roasted peanuts**

Prepare 1 cup rice according to package directions to yield about 3 cups cooked rice.

1. Bring large saucepan of water to a boil. Add broccoli; cook 4 minutes or until tender. Drain and set aside.

2. Stand tofu on long narrow end and cut into four slices. Turn onto large flat side; cut into quarters lengthwise, then cut in half crosswise to make 32 thin rectangles. Place in single layer on cutting board; press gently with paper towels to remove excess moisture. Season tofu with salt and pepper.

3. Place ½ cup cornstarch in medium bowl. Add tofu to cornstarch in batches; toss gently to coat. Heat 2 tablespoons oil in large nonstick skillet over medium-high heat. Working in batches, cook tofu in single layer about 5 minutes per side or until lightly browned, adding additional 1 tablespoon oil as needed.

4. Meanwhile, heat remaining 2 teaspoons oil in medium saucepan over medium-high heat. Add onion and garlic; cook and stir 2 to 3 minutes or until tender. Reduce heat to medium; stir in peanut butter, brown sugar, soy sauce, paprika and red pepper until smooth. Stir in coconut milk until well blended.* Bring to a simmer. Combine remaining 1 tablespoon cornstarch and 1 tablespoon water in small bowl; stir into sauce. Cook and stir 1 to 2 minutes or until sauce is thickened. Stir in lime juice.

5. Return all tofu to skillet. Pour in sauce; cook and stir over medium heat until tofu is coated, adding additional water by tablespoonfuls if sauce is too thick. Serve with rice and broccoli; garnish with peanuts.

**At this point, sauce may be cooled, covered and refrigerated up to 3 days in advance.*

Butternut Squash in Coconut Milk

makes 4 to 6 servings

- **⅓ cup flaked coconut**
- **2 teaspoons vegetable oil**
- **½ small onion, finely chopped**
- **2 cloves garlic, minced**
- **1 cup unsweetened coconut milk**
- **¼ cup packed brown sugar**
- **1 tablespoon soy sauce**
- **¼ teaspoon salt**
- **⅛ to ¼ teaspoon red pepper flakes**
- **1 butternut squash (about 2 pounds), peeled and cut into large cubes**
- **1 tablespoon chopped fresh cilantro**

1. Cook coconut in medium skillet over medium-low heat 5 to 7 minutes or until toasted, stirring frequently. Spread on plate to cool.
2. Heat oil in large saucepan over medium-high heat. Add onion and garlic; cook and stir 3 minutes or until tender. Add coconut milk, brown sugar, soy sauce, salt and red pepper flakes; stir until brown sugar is dissolved. Bring to a boil; stir in squash.
3. Reduce heat to medium; cover and simmer 30 minutes or until squash is tender. Transfer squash to serving bowl with slotted spoon.
4. Increase heat to high; boil cooking liquid until thick, stirring constantly. Pour liquid over squash in bowl; stir gently to blend. Sprinkle with toasted coconut and cilantro.

Ginger Tofu Bowl

makes 4 servings

- **7 tablespoons soy sauce, divided**
- **2 teaspoons minced fresh ginger**
- **1 teaspoon toasted sesame oil**
- **1 package (about 14 ounces) firm tofu, drained and cut into ½-inch cubes**
- **1 cup uncooked brown rice**
- **½ seedless cucumber, thinly sliced**
- **¼ teaspoon salt**
- **¼ teaspoon sugar**
- **¼ cup rice vinegar**
- **1 teaspoon vegetable oil**
- **1 package (8 ounces) sliced cremini or white mushrooms**
- **1 cup thawed frozen shelled edamame**
- **2 carrots, julienned or thinly sliced**
- **4 green onions, thinly sliced**
- **Pickled ginger**
- **Sesame seeds**

1. Combine 6 tablespoons soy sauce, ginger and sesame oil in large shallow bowl. Add tofu; stir to coat. Refrigerate 2 hours or overnight.
2. Prepare rice according to package directions.
3. Meanwhile, place cucumbers in shallow bowl. Sprinkle with salt and sugar; toss to coat. Add vinegar; mix well.
4. Heat vegetable oil in medium skillet over medium heat. Add mushrooms; cook and stir 5 minutes or until tender and lightly browned. Remove from heat; stir in remaining 1 tablespoon soy sauce.
5. Divide rice among four bowls. Arrange tofu, mushrooms, cucumbers, edamame and carrots over rice; top with green onions, pickled ginger and sesame seeds.

Buddha's Delight

makes 2 servings

- **1 package (1 ounce) dried black Chinese mushrooms**
- **1 package (about 14 ounces) firm tofu, drained**
- **1 tablespoon peanut or vegetable oil**
- **2 cups diagonally cut 1-inch asparagus pieces**
- **1 medium onion, cut into thin wedges**
- **2 cloves garlic, minced**
- **½ cup vegetable broth**
- **3 tablespoons hoisin sauce**
- **¼ cup coarsely chopped fresh cilantro or thinly sliced green onions**

1. Place mushrooms in medium bowl; cover with warm water. Soak about 30 minutes or until soft. Drain mushrooms, reserving soaking liquid. Discard stems; thinly slice caps.
2. Meanwhile, place tofu on plate or cutting board lined with paper towels; cover with additional paper towels. Place flat, heavy object on top; let stand 15 minutes. Cut tofu into ¾-inch cubes or triangles.
3. Heat oil in wok or large skillet over medium-high heat. Add asparagus, onion and garlic; stir-fry 4 minutes.
4. Add mushrooms, ¼ cup reserved mushroom liquid, broth and hoisin sauce; cook over medium heat 2 to 3 minutes or until asparagus is crisp-tender. Stir in tofu; cook until heated through. Sprinkle with cilantro.

Sticky Tofu

makes 4 servings

- **1 cup uncooked brown rice or medium-grain white rice**
- **¼ cup ketchup**
- **3 tablespoons soy sauce**
- **2 tablespoons packed brown sugar**
- **2 cloves garlic, minced**
- **1 package (about 14 ounces) firm or extra firm tofu, drained**
- **Salt and black pepper**
- **3 tablespoons cornstarch**
- **1 tablespoon vegetable oil**
- **1 head bok choy, sliced lengthwise ½-inch thick, then crosswise into thin slices**

1. Cook rice according to package directions; keep warm.
2. Combine ketchup, soy sauce, brown sugar and garlic in medium bowl; mix well. Cut tofu into cubes; pat dry with paper towels. Season with salt and pepper. Place cornstarch in large bowl; add tofu and toss gently to coat.
3. Heat oil in large skillet over medium-high heat. Add tofu; cook 5 minutes or until lightly browned, stirring occasionally. Add bok choy; cook and stir 5 minutes. Add sauce; cook and stir 5 to 7 minutes or until sauce is thickened and slightly caramelized. Serve over rice.

Mongolian Vegetables

makes 2 main-dish or 4 side-dish servings

- **1 package (about 14 ounces) firm tofu, drained**
- **4 tablespoons soy sauce, divided**
- **1 tablespoon toasted sesame oil**
- **1 large head bok choy (about 1½ pounds)**
- **2 teaspoons cornstarch**
- **1 tablespoon peanut or vegetable oil**
- **1 red or yellow bell pepper, cut into short, thin strips**
- **2 cloves garlic, minced**
- **4 green onions, cut into ½-inch pieces**
- **2 teaspoons sesame seeds, toasted***

****To toast sesame seeds, spread in small skillet. Shake skillet over medium-low heat 3 minutes or until seeds begin to pop and turn golden.***

1. Press tofu between paper towels to drain excess water; cut into ¾-inch squares. Place in shallow dish. Combine 2 tablespoons soy sauce and sesame oil in small bowl; drizzle over tofu. Let stand while preparing vegetables.
2. Cut stems from bok choy leaves; cut stems into ½-inch pieces. Cut leaves crosswise into ½-inch slices.
3. Stir remaining 2 tablespoons soy sauce into cornstarch in small bowl until smooth.
4. Heat peanut oil in wok or large skillet over medium-high heat. Add bok choy stems, bell pepper and garlic; stir-fry 5 minutes. Add bok choy leaves and green onions; stir-fry 2 minutes.
5. Add tofu mixture; stir-fry 2 minutes or until tofu is heated through. Stir cornstarch mixture; add to wok. Stir-fry 30 seconds or until sauce boils and thickens. Sprinkle with sesame seeds.

Tofu Satay with Peanut Sauce

makes 4 servings

Satay

- 1 package (about 14 ounces) firm tofu, drained and pressed*
- ⅓ cup water
- ⅓ cup soy sauce
- 1 tablespoon toasted sesame oil
- 1 teaspoon minced garlic
- 1 teaspoon minced fresh ginger
- 1 package (8 ounces) mushrooms, stemmed
- 1 red bell pepper, cut into 1-inch pieces

Peanut Sauce

- 1 can (about 13 ounces) unsweetened coconut milk
- ½ cup creamy peanut butter
- 2 tablespoons packed brown sugar
- 1 tablespoon rice vinegar
- 1 to 2 teaspoons red Thai curry paste

****Place tofu on paper towels in a colander in the sink. Place a small, flat plate on top of tofu and weigh it down with a large can. Let stand 30 minutes.***

1. Cut tofu into 24 cubes. Combine water, soy sauce, sesame oil, garlic and ginger in small bowl. Place tofu, mushrooms and bell pepper in large resealable food storage bag. Add soy sauce mixture; seal bag and turn gently to coat. Marinate 30 minutes, turning occasionally. Soak eight 8-inch bamboo skewers in water 20 minutes.
2. Preheat oven to 400°F. Spray 13×9-inch glass baking dish with nonstick cooking spray.
3. Drain tofu mixture; discard marinade. Alternately thread tofu, mushrooms and peppers onto skewers. Place skewers in prepared dish.
4. Bake 25 minutes or until tofu cubes are lightly browned and vegetables are softened.
5. Meanwhile for peanut sauce, whisk coconut milk, peanut butter, brown sugar, vinegar and curry paste in small saucepan over medium heat. Bring to a boil, stirring constantly. Reduce heat to low; cook 20 minutes or until creamy and thick, stirring frequently. Serve satay with sauce.

Noodles

Spicy Peanut Noodles

makes 2 to 4 servings

- **1 package (about 14 ounces) Asian stir-fry wheat noodles (hokkien, udon or chow mein)**
- **2½ tablespoons creamy peanut butter**
- **3 tablespoons water, plus additional if needed**
- **3 tablespoons soy sauce**
- **2 tablespoons unseasoned rice vinegar**
- **1 tablespoon packed brown sugar**
- **1 tablespoon minced fresh cilantro**
- **1 tablespoon chili oil**
- **¼ teaspoon red pepper flakes**
- **½ cucumber, julienned**
- **Fresh cilantro leaves**

1. Cook noodles according to package directions; drain.
2. Meanwhile, whisk peanut butter, 3 tablespoons water, soy sauce, vinegar, brown sugar, minced cilantro, chili oil and red pepper flakes in large bowl until smooth and well blended. Add noodles; stir until well coated, adding additional water if needed to thin sauce. Cover and refrigerate until cold.
3. Divide noodles among serving bowls. Top with cucumber and cilantro.

Note You can substitute 1 package (16 ounces) uncooked spaghetti or linguine for the Asian stir-fry noodles. Cook in a large saucepan of salted boiling water according to package directions for al dente. Drain and place in large bowl, reserving some of pasta cooking water to use in the sauce.

Jap Chae (Korean Glass Noodle Stir-Fry)

makes 6 servings

- **5 ounces cellophane noodles (bean threads)**
- **¼ cup soy sauce**
- **1½ tablespoons toasted sesame oil**
- **3 cloves garlic, minced**
- **2 teaspoons sugar**
- **2 tablespoons vegetable oil**
- **1 sweet potato, spiral-sliced* or julienned**
- **1 large carrot, peeled and julienned**
- **1 small red onion, halved and thinly sliced**
- **1 small red bell pepper, julienned**
- **1 cup fresh shiitake mushrooms, stemmed and sliced**
- **3 green onions, sliced**
- **1 tablespoon sesame seeds, toasted**

Use a spiralizer with the thin ribbon blade to spiral the sweet potato; cut into desired lengths.

1 Soak noodles in hot water according to package directions. Whisk soy sauce, sesame oil, garlic and sugar in small bowl.

2 Heat vegetable oil in large skillet over high heat. Add sweet potato; cook and stir 3 minutes. Add carrot, onion, bell pepper and mushrooms; cook and stir 5 minutes or until vegetables are tender. Drain noodles; add to skillet with soy sauce mixture. Cook 2 minutes or until sauce is absorbed. Stir in green onions and sesame seeds. Serve warm, cold or at room temperature.

Note This classic Korean dish is typically made with sweet potato noodles (dangmyeon). In this version, chewy cellophane noodles are mixed with ribbons of fresh sweet potato. Leftover noodles make great lunches because they're good served cold, and their flavor gets even better with more time to blend.

Vegetarian Rice Noodles

makes 4 servings

- **½ cup soy sauce**
- **⅓ cup sugar**
- **¼ cup lime juice**
- **2 fresh red Thai chiles *or* 1 large jalapeño pepper, finely chopped**
- **8 ounces rice vermicelli (thin rice noodles)**
- **¼ cup vegetable oil**
- **8 ounces firm tofu, drained and cut into triangles**
- **1 jicama (8 ounces), peeled and chopped *or* 1 can (8 ounces) sliced water chestnuts, drained**
- **2 medium sweet potatoes (1 pound), peeled and cut into ¼-inch-thick slices**
- **2 large leeks, cut into ¼-inch-thick slices**
- **¼ cup chopped dry-roasted peanuts**
- **2 tablespoons chopped fresh mint**
- **2 tablespoons chopped fresh cilantro**

1. Combine soy sauce, sugar, lime juice and chiles in small bowl until well blended; set aside.
2. Place rice noodles in medium bowl. Cover with hot water; let stand 15 minutes or until soft. Drain well; cut into 3-inch lengths.
3. Meanwhile, heat oil in large skillet over medium-high heat. Add tofu; cook 4 minutes per side or until golden brown. Drain on paper towel-lined baking sheet.
4. Add jicama to skillet; stir-fry 5 minutes or until lightly browned. Remove to baking sheet. Stir-fry sweet potatoes in batches until tender and browned. Remove to baking sheet. Add leeks to skillet; stir-fry 1 minute. Remove to baking sheet.
5. Stir soy sauce mixture; add to skillet. Cook until sugar dissolves. Add noodles; toss to coat. Gently stir in tofu, vegetables, peanuts, mint and cilantro.

Japanese Pan Noodles

makes 4 to 6 servings

- ⅓ cup soy sauce
- ⅓ cup packed brown sugar
- 1 tablespoon mirin
- 1 teaspoon chili garlic sauce
- 1 tablespoon vegetable or peanut oil
- 2 cups small broccoli florets (about 2 small crowns or 10 ounces)
- 2 cups sliced mushrooms
- 1 cup matchstick carrots (about 2 medium) or shredded carrots
- 1 tablespoon finely chopped fresh ginger
- 1 package (14 to 16 ounces) cooked udon noodles*
- Black sesame seeds
- Fresh cilantro sprigs (optional)

***Or substitute 1 package (16 ounces) dried or fresh udon noodles; cook and drain according to package directions.**

1 Combine soy sauce and brown sugar in small saucepan; bring to a boil over medium-high heat. Reduce heat to medium; cook about 10 minutes or until reduced and thickened slightly, stirring frequently. Remove from heat; stir in mirin and chili garlic sauce until well blended.

2 Heat oil in wok or large saucepan over high heat. Add broccoli and mushrooms; cook and stir about 5 minutes or until vegetables are crisp-tender. Add carrots and ginger; cook and stir 1 minute. Add soy sauce mixture and noodles; cook 3 to 5 minutes or until noodles are heated through and most of sauce is absorbed, stirring frequently.

3 Sprinkle with sesame seeds; garnish with cilantro.

Basil Chicken with Rice Noodles

makes 4 servings

- **1 pound boneless skinless chicken breasts, cut into bite-size pieces**
- **5 tablespoons soy sauce, divided**
- **1 tablespoon white wine or rice wine (optional)**
- **3 cloves garlic, minced**
- **1 tablespoon grated fresh ginger**
- **8 ounces uncooked rice noodles**
- **1 red onion, sliced**
- **1 yellow or red bell pepper, cut into strips**
- **2 medium carrots, cut into matchstick-size pieces**
- **2 jalapeño or serrano peppers, seeded and chopped**
- **Juice of 2 limes**
- **2 tablespoons packed brown sugar**
- **1 cup loosely packed basil leaves, shredded**
- **1 tablespoon vegetable oil**

1. Place chicken in shallow dish. Combine 3 tablespoons soy sauce, wine, if desired, garlic and ginger in small bowl. Pour over chicken and stir to coat. Marinate at room temperature 30 minutes or refrigerate up to 2 hours.
2. Place noodles in large bowl. Cover with hot water; let stand 15 minutes or until tender. Drain.
3. Combine onion, bell pepper, carrots and jalapeño peppers in medium bowl. Whisk remaining 2 tablespoons soy sauce, lime juice and brown sugar in small bowl until sugar is dissolved. Coarsely shred basil and place in medium bowl.
4. Heat oil in large skillet or wok over medium-high heat. Add chicken with marinade; cook and stir 5 minutes or until cooked through. Add vegetables; cook and stir 4 to 6 minutes or until vegetables are crisp-tender.
5. Stir sauce and add to skillet; cook and stir 2 minutes. Add rice noodles and basil; toss to combine.

Bangkok Peanut Noodles

makes 4 servings

Sauce

- 6 tablespoons peanut butter
- ¼ cup soy sauce
- 1 tablespoon unseasoned rice vinegar
- 1 tablespoon packed brown sugar
- 1 tablespoon sriracha sauce
- 2 teaspoons grated fresh ginger
- 2 cloves garlic, minced
- 2 teaspoons toasted sesame oil

Stir-Fry

- 1 package (6 ounces) dried chow mein stir-fry noodles
- 1 pound boneless skinless chicken breasts, cut into 1-inch pieces *or* 1 package (14 ounces) extra firm tofu, cut into ½-inch cubes
- ½ cup cornstarch
- 3 tablespoons vegetable oil, divided
- 1 red bell pepper, cut into thin strips
- ½ medium onion, thinly sliced
- 2 cups sliced Swiss chard or bok choy
- Chopped roasted peanuts (optional)

1. For sauce, whisk peanut butter, soy sauce, vinegar, brown sugar, sriracha, ginger, garlic and sesame oil in small bowl until smooth.

2. For stir-fry, cook noodles according to package directions; drain and rinse under cold water until cool.

3. Combine chicken and cornstarch in medium bowl; toss to coat. Heat 2 tablespoons vegetable oil in large skillet over medium-high heat. Add chicken; stir-fry 5 minutes or until chicken is golden brown and cooked through. Drain on paper towel-lined plate. Wipe out skillet with paper towel.

4. Heat remaining 1 tablespoon vegetable oil in same skillet over high heat. Add bell pepper and onion; stir-fry 5 minutes or until browned. Add chard; stir-fry 1 minute or until wilted. Add noodles and sauce; cook and stir until noodles are coated with sauce. Add 1 tablespoon water, if needed, to loosen sauce. Return chicken to skillet; stir to coat. Cook just until heated through. Garnish with peanuts.

Rice Noodles with Broccoli & Tofu

makes 4 servings

1 package (8 to 10 ounces) wide rice noodles
1 package (about 14 ounces) firm or extra firm tofu
Salt and black pepper
2 tablespoons peanut or vegetable oil
3 medium shallots, sliced
6 cloves garlic, minced
1 jalapeño pepper, minced
2 teaspoons minced fresh ginger
3 cups broccoli florets
¼ cup soy sauce
1 to 2 tablespoons fish sauce*
Fresh basil leaves (optional)

To make this dish vegetarian, look for vegetarian fish sauce or substitute additional soy sauce or fresh lime juice.

1 Place noodles in medium bowl. Cover with hot water; let stand 15 minutes or until tender. Drain.

2 Meanwhile, drain tofu and press between paper towels to remove excess water. Cut tofu into bite-size pieces. Season with salt and black pepper.

3 Heat oil in large skillet or wok over medium-high heat. Add tofu; cook 5 minutes or until tofu is lightly browned on all sides, stirring occasionally. Drain tofu on paper towel-lined plate.

4 Add shallots, garlic, jalapeño and ginger to skillet; stir-fry 2 to 3 minutes. Add broccoli; stir-fry 1 minute. Cover and cook 3 minutes or until broccoli is crisp-tender. Add tofu, noodles, soy sauce and fish sauce to skillet; stir-fry 8 minutes or until heated through. Garnish with basil.

Szechuan Cold Noodles

makes 4 servings

- **8 ounces uncooked vermicelli, broken in half, or Chinese egg noodles**
- **3 tablespoons unseasoned rice vinegar**
- **3 tablespoons soy sauce**
- **2 tablespoons peanut or vegetable oil**
- **1 clove garlic, minced**
- **1 teaspoon minced fresh ginger**
- **1 teaspoon toasted sesame oil**
- **½ teaspoon crushed Szechuan peppercorns or red pepper flakes**
- **¼ cup coarsely chopped fresh cilantro (optional)**
- **¼ cup chopped peanuts**

1 Cook noodles in large saucepan of salted boiling water according to package directions; drain.

2 Whisk vinegar, soy sauce, peanut oil, garlic, ginger, sesame oil and peppercorns in large bowl; mix well. Add hot cooked noodles; toss to coat. Sprinkle with cilantro, if desired, and peanuts. Refrigerate until cold.

Szechuan Vegetable Noodles Add 1 cup chopped peeled cucumber, ½ cup chopped red bell pepper, ½ cup sliced green onions and an additional 1 tablespoon soy sauce.

Mushroom Noodle Stir-Fry

makes 4 servings

- **8 ounces uncooked Chinese egg noodles or spaghetti**
- **8 ounces shiitake mushrooms, stemmed and thinly sliced (¼-inch slices)**
- **Pinch of salt**
- **2 tablespoons butter**
- **1 tablespoon minced garlic**
- **2 teaspoons honey**
- **½ cup stir-fry sauce**
- **2 to 3 tablespoons water**
- **2 green onions, sliced diagonally**

1. Cook noodles according to package directions; drain and rinse under cold water to stop cooking.
2. Heat large skillet over medium-high heat. Add mushrooms and salt; cook and stir about 5 minutes or until browned. Add butter, garlic and honey; cook and stir 1 minute or until butter is melted and garlic is fragrant but not browned. Add stir-fry sauce, 2 tablespoons water and noodles; cook and stir 2 to 3 minutes or until heated through. Add additional water by teaspoonfuls to loosen sauce, if necessary.
3. Divide noodles between serving bowls; top with green onions.

Sesame Noodles

makes 6 to 8 servings

- 1 package (16 ounces) uncooked spaghetti
- 6 tablespoons soy sauce
- 5 tablespoons toasted sesame oil
- 3 tablespoons sugar
- 3 tablespoons unseasoned rice vinegar
- 2 tablespoons vegetable oil
- 3 cloves garlic, minced
- 1 teaspoon grated fresh ginger
- ½ teaspoon sriracha
- 2 green onions, sliced
- 1 red bell pepper
- 1 cucumber
- 1 carrot
- Sesame seeds (optional)

1 Cook spaghetti in large saucepan of boiling salted water according to package directions until for al dente. Drain, reserving 2 tablespoons pasta cooking water.

2 Whisk soy sauce, sesame oil, sugar, vinegar, vegetable oil, garlic, ginger, sriracha and reserved pasta water in large bowl. Stir in noodles and green onions. Let stand at least 30 minutes until noodles have cooled to room temperature and most of sauce is absorbed, stirring occasionally.

3 Meanwhile, cut bell pepper into thin strips. Peel cucumber and carrot and shred with julienne peeler into long strands, or cut into thin strips. Stir into noodles. Serve at room temperature or refrigerate until ready to serve. Top with sesame seeds, if desired.

Rice

Sushi Rice

makes 3 cups

- **1 cup uncooked Japanese short grain sushi rice***
- **1¼ cups water**
- **½ teaspoon salt**
- **2 tablespoons unseasoned rice vinegar****
- **4 teaspoons sugar**

If you can't find white rice labeled "sushi rice," use Calrose or any short grain white rice instead.

*****Or use seasoned rice vinegar and skip adding sugar and salt.***

1 Rinse rice in fine-mesh strainer under cold water until water runs clear. Drain thoroughly. Place rice in medium saucepan with 1¼ cups water and salt. Bring to a boil; stir. Reduce heat to very low; cover and cook 20 minutes or until water is absorbed. *Do not lift lid while cooking.* Remove from heat; let stand 5 minutes.

2 Combine rice vinegar and sugar in small microwavable bowl or measuring cup. Heat 30 seconds and stir to dissolve sugar.

3 Transfer rice to shallow wooden or glass bowl using wooden spoon. Drizzle with vinegar mixture; fold into rice gently, taking care not to crush or break rice grains.

4 Serve immediately as a side dish or cool completely to use for sushi. Do not refrigerate before making sushi or rice will become gummy and hard to work with.

Spicy Fried Rice with Tofu

makes 4 servings

- **2 eggs**
- **1 tablespoon plus 1½ teaspoons vegetable oil, divided**
- **1 tablespoon minced garlic**
- **1 tablespoon minced fresh ginger**
- **½ teaspoon red pepper flakes**
- **2 cups thinly sliced napa cabbage**
- **1 cup chopped carrots**
- **1 cup thawed frozen green peas**
- **3 cups cooked white rice***
- **4 ounces firm tofu, drained and cut into ½-inch cubes**
- **¼ cup vegetable broth**
- **¼ cup soy sauce**
- **3 tablespoons dry sherry**
- **2 teaspoons balsamic vinegar**

Prepare 1 cup rice according to package directions to yield about 3 cups cooked rice. Refrigerate overnight or until cold.

1. Lightly beat eggs in small bowl. Heat 1½ teaspoons oil in wok or large skillet over medium-high heat. Add eggs; cook without stirring 2 to 3 minutes or until set. Remove from wok; cut into small pieces.

2. Heat remaining 1 tablespoon oil in same wok over high heat. Add garlic, ginger and red pepper flakes; cook 30 seconds or until fragrant. Add cabbage, carrots and peas; cook 5 to 10 minutes or until carrots are crisp-tender.

3. Stir in rice, tofu, broth, soy sauce, sherry and vinegar; cook and stir 3 minutes. Remove from heat. Stir in eggs.

Three-Topped Rice

makes 4 servings

- **1 ounce Pickled Ginger (page 149, optional) or jarred pickled ginger**
- **2½ cups uncooked short grain rice**
- **4¼ cups water, divided**
- **1 teaspoon salt**
- **2 tablespoons sugar, divided**
- **2 tablespoons sake or dry sherry, divided**
- **1 tablespoon plus 1 teaspoon soy sauce, divided**
- **1 teaspoon grated fresh ginger**
- **8 ounces ground chicken**
- **4 eggs, lightly beaten**
- **1½ cups thawed frozen green peas**

1. Prepare Pickled Ginger, if desired; cut into thin strips; set aside.
2. Rinse rice in fine-mesh strainer under cold water until water runs clear. Drain thoroughly. Place rice in medium saucepan with 2¾ cups water and salt. Bring to a boil; stir. Reduce heat to very low; cover and cook 20 minutes or until water is absorbed. *Do not lift lid while cooking.* Remove from heat; let stand 5 minutes.
3. Gently fluff rice with wooden spoon. Lay dry kitchen towel over saucepan; replace lid. Let stand 10 minutes to absorb excess moisture.
4. Combine 1 tablespoon sugar, 1 tablespoon sake, 1 tablespoon soy sauce and ginger in medium saucepan; bring to a boil over high heat. Add chicken; cook and stir 3 to 4 minutes or until chicken is no longer pink; remove from heat.
5. Place eggs, remaining 1 tablespoon sugar, 1 tablespoon sake and 1 teaspoon soy sauce in medium skillet. Cook 3 to 5 minutes over medium-low heat until eggs are set but still moist, stirring constantly. Remove from heat.
6. Divide rice among four serving bowls; top with chicken, peas and eggs. Garnish with Pickled Ginger.

Pickled Ginger Cut 4 ounces peeled fresh ginger crosswise into very thin slices. Place in small bowl; add 1 cup boiling water. Let stand 30 seconds; drain well. Place ½ cup rice vinegar, 2 tablespoons sugar and ½ teaspoon salt in small bowl; stir until sugar is dissolved. Add ginger; stir to coat well. Cover bowl; let stand at room temperature at least 1 hour. Refrigerate until cold.

Spicy Tuna Sushi Bowl

makes 2 servings

- ¼ **cup mayonnaise**
- 4 **teaspoons unseasoned rice vinegar, divided**
- 2 **teaspoons sriracha or hot chile sauce**
- 1 **tuna steak (about 6 ounces)**
- 1½ **cups hot cooked brown rice**
- ½ **cup diced cucumber**
- ½ **ripe avocado, sliced**
- **Black sesame seeds (optional)**

1. Whisk mayonnaise, 2 teaspoons vinegar and sriracha sauce and in small bowl. Rub 1 tablespoon sauce evenly over tuna; marinate 10 minutes.
2. Meanwhile, stir remaining 2 teaspoons vinegar into rice; set aside.
3. Heat small nonstick skillet over medium high heat. Cook tuna 2 minutes per side for medium-rare or until desired doneness. Slice tuna.
4. Divide rice, cucumber, avocado and tuna slices between two bowls. Sprinkle evenly with sesame seeds, if desired. Serve with remaining sauce.

Chicken Fried Rice

makes 4 servings

- **12 ounces boneless skinless chicken breasts, cut into ½-inch cubes**
- **Salt and black pepper**
- **2 tablespoons vegetable oil, divided**
- **2 tablespoons butter**
- **2 cloves garlic, minced**
- **½ sweet onion, diced**
- **1 medium carrot, diced**
- **2 green onions, thinly sliced**
- **3 eggs**
- **4 cups cooked rice***
- **3 tablespoons soy sauce**
- **2 tablespoons sesame seeds**

For rice, cook 1½ cups rice according to package directions without oil or butter. Spread hot rice on large rimmed baking sheet; cool to room temperature. Refrigerate several hours or overnight. Measure 4 cups for recipe.

1. Season chicken all over with salt and pepper. Heat 1 tablespoon oil in large skillet over medium-high heat. Add chicken; cook and stir 5 to 6 minutes or until cooked through. Add butter and garlic; cook and stir 1 minute or until butter is melted. Remove to medium bowl.

2. Add sweet onion, carrot and green onions to skillet; cook and stir over high heat 3 minutes or until vegetables are softened. Add to bowl with chicken.

3. Heat remaining 1 tablespoon oil in same skillet. Crack eggs into skillet; cook and stir 45 seconds or until eggs are scrambled but still moist. Return chicken and vegetables to skillet with rice, soy sauce and sesame seeds; cook and stir 2 minutes or until well blended and heated through. Season with additional salt and pepper.

Chicken Congee

makes 6 servings

- 6 cups water
- 4 cups chicken broth
- 4 chicken drumsticks
- 1 cup white jasmine rice, rinsed and drained
- 1 (1-inch) piece ginger, sliced into 4 pieces
- 2 teaspoons salt
- ¼ teaspoon ground white pepper
- Optional toppings: soy sauce, toasted sesame oil, thinly sliced green onions, fried shallots, fried garlic slices, salted roasted peanuts and pickled vegetables

Slow Cooker Directions

1. Combine water, broth, chicken, rice, ginger, salt and pepper in slow cooker. Cover; cook on LOW 8 hours or on HIGH 4 hours or until rice has completely broken down and mixture is thickened.

2. Remove and discard ginger. Remove chicken to large cutting board. Discard skin and bones. Shred chicken using two forks. Stir chicken back into slow cooker. Ladle congee into serving bowls; top with desired toppings.

Fried Rice with Shrimp

makes 6 servings

- **2 tablespoons vegetable oil**
- **3 green onions, chopped**
- **1 clove garlic, minced**
- **2 eggs, lightly beaten**
- **3 cups cooked rice, chilled or at room temperature**
- **4 ounces cooked shrimp, chopped***
- **3 tablespoons soy sauce**
- **1 teaspoon sugar**

****Or substitute cooked ham, beef, pork or chicken.***

1 Heat wok or large skillet over medium heat. Add oil; heat until oil shimmers. Add green onions and garlic; cook and stir 1 minute. Add egg; cook and stir until scrambled.

2 Add rice; cook and stir 2 to 3 minutes or until heated through. Stir in shrimp, soy sauce and sugar; cook and stir 1 to 2 minutes or until heated through.

Tip Making fried rice is a great way to use up leftover rice. In fact, when you're cooking rice, plan ahead and make extra rice to chill for fried rice dishes.

Curries

Green Curry with Tofu

makes 2 to 4 servings

- 1 tablespoon vegetable oil
- 1 onion, chopped
- 1 package (about 14 ounces) firm tofu, drained and cut into 1-inch cubes
- ⅓ cup Thai green curry paste
- 1 can (about 13 ounces) unsweetened coconut milk
- 1 broccoli crown (about 8 ounces), cut into florets
- 1 cup cut green beans (1-inch pieces)
- ½ teaspoon salt
- Hot cooked brown rice or rice noodles

1. Heat oil in large skillet or wok over high heat. Add onion; cook and stir 5 minutes or until softened and lightly browned.
2. Add tofu and curry paste; cook and stir 2 minutes or until curry is fragrant and tofu is coated. Add coconut milk; bring to a boil. Add broccoli and green beans.
3. Reduce heat to low; cook 20 minutes or until vegetables are tender and sauce is thickened, stirring frequently. Season with salt. Serve over rice.

Tofu, Vegetable & Curry Stir-Fry

makes 4 servings

- 1 package (about 14 ounces) extra firm tofu, cut into ¾-inch cubes
- ¾ cup unsweetened coconut milk
- 2 tablespoons lime juice
- 1 tablespoon curry powder
- 2 teaspoons toasted sesame oil
- 2 tablespoons vegetable oil
- 4 cups broccoli florets (1½-inch pieces)
- 2 red bell peppers, cut into short, thin strips
- 1 red onion, cut into thin wedges
- ¼ teaspoon salt
- 3 cups hot cooked rice*

**Prepare 1 cup rice according to package directions to yield about 3 cups cooked rice.*

1. Press tofu cubes between layers of paper towels to remove excess moisture. Combine coconut milk, lime juice, curry powder and sesame oil in medium bowl.
2. Heat 1 tablespoon vegetable oil in large nonstick skillet over medium heat. Add tofu; cook 10 minutes or until lightly browned on all sides, turning occasionally. Remove to plate.
3. Heat remaining 1 tablespoon vegetable oil in same skillet over high heat. Add broccoli, bell peppers and onion; stir-fry about 5 minutes or until vegetables are crisp-tender. Return tofu to skillet; add coconut milk mixture. Bring to a boil, stirring frequently. Stir in salt. Serve with rice, if desired.

Thai Shrimp Curry

makes 4 servings

- **1 can (about 13 ounces) unsweetened coconut milk, divided**
- **⅓ cup water**
- **1 tablespoon packed brown sugar**
- **1 tablespoon Thai red curry paste**
- **1 tablespoon fish sauce**
- **Peel of 1 lime, finely chopped**
- **1 pound large raw shrimp, peeled and deveined**
- **½ cup fresh basil leaves, thinly sliced**
- **½ cup chopped roasted peanuts (optional)**
- **3 cups hot cooked jasmine rice***

Prepare 1 cup rice according to package directions to yield about 3 cups cooked rice.

1. Bring coconut milk to a boil in large skillet over medium heat, stirring occasionally. Add water, brown sugar, curry paste, fish sauce and lime peel. Reduce heat to medium-low. Cook 10 to 15 minutes or until sauce thickens slightly, stirring frequently.

2. Reduce heat to low. Stir in shrimp and basil; cook 3 to 5 minutes or until shrimp turn pink and opaque. Stir in peanuts, if desired. Serve over rice.

Thai Veggie Curry

makes 4 servings

- **2 tablespoons vegetable oil**
- **1 onion, quartered and thinly sliced**
- **1 tablespoon Thai red curry paste (or to taste)**
- **1 can (about 13 ounces) unsweetened coconut milk**
- **2 red or yellow bell peppers, cut into strips**
- **1½ cups cauliflower and/or broccoli florets**
- **1 cup pea pods**
- **1 package (about 14 ounces) tofu, pressed* and cubed**
- **Salt and pepper**
- **¼ cup slivered fresh basil**
- **3 cups hot cooked jasmine rice****

Cut tofu in half horizontally and place it between layers of paper towels. Place a weighted cutting board on top; let stand 15 to 30 minutes.

*****Prepare 1 cup rice according to package directions to yield about 3 cups cooked rice.***

1. Heat oil in wok or large skillet over medium-high heat. Add onion; cook and stir 5 minutes or until softened. Add curry paste; cook and stir to coat onion. Add coconut milk; bring to a boil, stirring to dissolve curry paste.
2. Add bell peppers and cauliflower; simmer over medium heat 4 to 5 minutes or until crisp-tender. Stir in pea pods; simmer 2 minutes. Gently stir in tofu; cook until heated through. Season to taste with salt and black pepper.
3. Sprinkle with basil; serve with rice.

Sweet Chicken Curry

makes 4 servings

- **1 pound boneless skinless chicken breasts, cut into 1-inch pieces**
- **1 large green or red bell pepper, cut into 1-inch pieces**
- **1 large onion, sliced**
- **1 large tomato, seeded and chopped**
- **½ cup prepared mango chutney**
- **¼ cup water**
- **2 tablespoons cornstarch**
- **1½ teaspoons curry powder**
- **3 cups hot cooked rice***

Prepare 1 cup rice according to package directions to yield about 3 cups cooked rice.

Slow Cooker Directions

1. Place chicken, bell pepper and onion in slow cooker. Top with tomato.
2. Mix chutney, water, cornstarch and curry powder in small bowl. Pour over chicken.
3. Cover; cook on LOW 3½ to 4½ hours or until chicken is tender. Serve over rice.

Asian Influence

Spicy Orange Chicken Nuggets

makes 4 to 6 servings

- 1 bag (28 ounces) frozen popcorn chicken bites
- 1½ cups honey teriyaki marinade
- ¾ cup orange juice concentrate
- ⅔ cup water
- 1 tablespoon orange marmalade
- ¾ teaspoon hot chile sauce or sriracha
- Thinly sliced green onions (optional)
- 3 cups hot cooked rice*

**Prepare 1 cup rice according to package directions to yield about 3 cups cooked rice.*

Slow Cooker Directions

1. Preheat oven to 450°F. Spread chicken evenly on baking sheet. Bake 12 to 14 minutes or until crisp. (Do not brown.) Transfer to slow cooker.
2. Combine teriyaki marinade, juice concentrate, water, marmalade and chile sauce in medium bowl. Pour over chicken. Cover; cook on LOW 3 to 3½ hours. Sprinkle with green onions, if desired. Serve with rice.

Sesame Chicken Salad Wonton Cups

makes 10 servings

20 (3-inch) wonton wrappers
8 ounces boneless skinless chicken breasts
1 cup fresh green beans, cut diagonally into ½-inch pieces
¼ cup mayonnaise
1 tablespoon toasted sesame seeds*
1 tablespoon chopped fresh cilantro
2 teaspoons honey
1 teaspoon soy sauce
⅛ teaspoon ground red pepper

****To toast sesame seeds, cook in single layer in heavy skillet over medium heat 2 minutes or until golden, stirring frequently.***

1 Preheat oven to 350°F. Spray mini (1¾-inch) muffin cups with cooking spray. Press one wonton wrapper into each muffin cup; spray with cooking spray. Bake 8 to 10 minutes or until golden brown. Cool completely in pan on wire rack.

2 Meanwhile, bring 2 cups water to a boil in medium saucepan. Add chicken. Reduce heat to low; cover and simmer 10 minutes or until chicken is cooked through (165°F), adding green beans after 7 minutes. Transfer chicken to cutting board; drain green beans.

3 Finely chop chicken when cool enough to handle. Place in medium bowl. Add green beans, mayonnaise, sesame seeds, cilantro, honey, soy sauce and red pepper. Divide chicken salad evenly among wonton cups.

Chop Suey Burgers

makes 4 servings

- **1 pound ground turkey**
- **¼ cup chopped red onion**
- **4 stalks celery, trimmed, peeled and chopped**
- **1 cup fresh or canned bean sprouts**
- **½ red bell pepper, finely chopped**
- **¼ cup canned sliced water chestnuts, drained and chopped**
- **2 tablespoons soy sauce**
- **½ teaspoon black pepper**
- **2 tablespoons vegetable oil**
- **¼ cup water**
- **1 cup chow mein noodles**

1. Combine turkey, onion, celery, sprouts, bell pepper, water chestnuts, soy sauce and black pepper in medium bowl. Shape into four patties.
2. Heat oil in large nonstick skillet over medium heat. Cook patties 12 minutes or until cooked through (165°F), turning once. Add water; cover and cook 2 minutes.
3. Place burgers on serving plates; top with chow mein noodles.

Asian Sweet Potato & Corn Stew

makes 6 servings

- 1 tablespoon vegetable oil
- 1 large onion, chopped
- 2 tablespoons minced fresh ginger
- ½ jalapeño or serrano pepper, seeded and minced
- 2 cloves garlic, minced
- 1 cup drained canned or thawed frozen corn
- 2 teaspoons curry powder
- 1 can (about 13 ounces) unsweetened coconut milk
- 1 teaspoon cornstarch
- 1 can (about 14 ounces) vegetable broth
- 1 tablespoon soy sauce, plus more to taste
- 4 sweet potatoes, peeled and cut into ¾-inch cubes
- 3 cups hot cooked rice*
- Chopped dry roasted peanuts and fresh cilantro (optional)

****Prepare 1 cup rice according to package directions to yield about 3 cups cooked rice.***

Slow Cooker Directions

1. Heat oil in large skillet over medium heat. Add onion, ginger, jalapeño and garlic; cook and stir 5 minutes or until onion is softened. Remove from heat. Stir in corn and curry powder.

2. Whisk coconut milk and cornstarch in slow cooker. Stir in broth and 1 tablespoon soy sauce. Add sweet potatoes and corn mixture. Cover; cook on LOW 5 to 6 hours or until sweet potatoes are tender.

3. Carefully stir gently to smooth cooking liquid (coconut milk may look curdled) without breaking up sweet potatoes. Stir in additional soy sauce to taste, if desired. Serve with rice, peanuts and cilantro.

Teriyaki Meat Loaf

makes 4 to 6 servings

- **1 tablespoon vegetable oil**
- **1 package (8 ounces) thinly sliced mushrooms**
- **½ cup chopped green onions**
- **1 package (3 ounces) ramen noodles, crushed***
- **½ cup teriyaki sauce**
- **1 egg, lightly beaten**
- **1½ pounds (24 ounces) ground beef**

****Use any flavor; discard seasoning packet.***

1. Preheat oven to 375°F.
2. Heat oil in medium skillet over medium-high heat. Add mushrooms; cook and stir 10 minutes or until softened. Add green onions; cook and stir 1 minute. Transfer to large bowl. Add noodles, teriyaki sauce and egg; stir well. Fold in beef. Press mixture into 8×4-inch loaf pan.
3. Bake 35 to 40 minutes or until cooked through (160°F). Let stand 10 minutes before slicing.

Thai Noodle Wraps

makes 8 wraps

- **1 package (3 ounces) chicken-flavored ramen noodles**
- **2 teaspoons creamy peanut butter**
- **1½ cups packaged coleslaw mix**
- **½ cup diced cooked chicken**
- **8 (6-inch) flour tortillas**
- **Soy sauce**

1. Cook noodles according to package directions; drain and return to saucepan. Add peanut butter, stirring until melted. Stir in coleslaw mix and chicken; cover and set aside 2 minutes.
2. Spoon noodle mixture onto tortillas. Drizzle with soy sauce. Roll up and serve immediately.

Egg Foo Yung

makes 2 main-dish or 4 side-dish servings

- **2 eggs**
- **2 egg whites**
- **½ cup fresh or canned bean sprouts, rinsed and drained**
- **½ cup chopped fresh mushrooms**
- **2 tablespoons thinly sliced green onion**
- **2 tablespoons soy sauce, divided**
- **1 tablespoon peanut or vegetable oil**
- **1 cup chicken broth**
- **1 tablespoon cornstarch**
- **¼ teaspoon sugar**
- **¼ teaspoon black pepper**

1 Beat eggs and egg whites in large bowl. Stir in bean sprouts, mushrooms, green onion and 1 tablespoon soy sauce.

2 Heat oil in large nonstick skillet over medium-high heat. Working in batches, add ¼ cupfuls egg mixture to skillet (egg mixture will run; do not crowd skillet). Cook 1 to 2 minutes or until bottoms are set. Turn over; cook 1 to 2 minutes or until cooked through. Remove to large plate; keep warm. Repeat with remaining egg mixture.

3 Whisk broth, remaining 1 tablespoon soy sauce and cornstarch in small bowl until smooth and well blended; add to skillet. Stir in sugar and pepper; cook and stir 1 minute or until sauce boils and thickens. Pour sauce over warm pancakes; serve immediately.

Variation Add ½ cup chopped cooked shrimp or ½ cup diced roasted pork to egg mixture.

Sweet & Sour Glazed Beef Kabobs

makes 6 servings

- **¾ cup cola beverage, divided**
- **½ cup pineapple juice**
- **¼ cup soy sauce**
- **⅓ cup cider vinegar**
- **1 tablespoon Worcestershire sauce**
- **1 tablespoon tomato paste**
- **4 tablespoons packed brown sugar, divided**
- **1 tablespoon garlic powder**
- **½ teaspoon red pepper flakes**
- **2 pounds boneless sirloin steak, cut into 1½-inch cubes**
- **1 large onion, cut into 1-inch pieces**
- **2½ teaspoons cornstarch**
- **2 to 3 teaspoons chili-garlic sauce**
- **Salt and black pepper**
- **Hot cooked white rice (optional)**

1 For marinade, combine ½ cup cola, pineapple juice, soy sauce, vinegar, Worcestershire sauce, tomato paste, 2 tablespoons brown sugar, garlic powder and red pepper flakes in medium bowl; mix well.

2 Combine steak and onion in large resealable food storage bag. Add marinade; seal bag and turn to coat. Marinate in refrigerator overnight.

3 Remove steak and onion from marinade. Pour marinade into small saucepan; bring to a boil over high heat. Stir 2 tablespoons hot marinade into cornstarch in small bowl until smooth. Stir cornstarch mixture into saucepan with remaining ¼ cup cola, 2 tablespoons brown sugar and chili-garlic sauce. Reduce heat to medium; cook 15 to 18 minutes or until sauce is thickened and reduced to 1 cup. Season to taste with salt and black pepper.

4 Meanwhile, preheat broiler. Line broiler pan or baking sheet with foil. Soak six wooden skewers in water 20 minutes. Alternately thread steak and onion onto skewers.

5 Broil kabobs 3 minutes, turn and broil 2 minutes. Brush kabobs generously with sauce. Serve over rice, if desired.

Korean Scallion Pancake Waffles

makes 4 servings

Dipping Sauce

- **3 tablespoons soy sauce**
- **1½ tablespoons water**
- **2 teaspoons unseasoned rice vinegar**
- **2 teaspoons toasted sesame oil**
- **1½ teaspoons sesame seeds**
- **¾ teaspoon sugar**
- **½ teaspoon minced garlic**

Waffles

- **¾ cup all-purpose flour**
- **½ cup cornstarch**
- **½ teaspoon salt**
- **1 cup ice cold water**
- **1 egg, lightly beaten**
- **½ red bell pepper, thinly sliced into 2-inch pieces**
- **¾ cup thinly sliced green onions, cut on bias into 2-inch lengths**
- **2 small carrots, peeled and grated (about ¾ cup)**
- **2 teaspoons minced garlic**
- **2 teaspoons vegetable oil, plus additional for brushing**

1. Preheat classic round waffle maker to medium-high heat. Set wire rack on top of large baking sheet.
2. For sauce, whisk soy sauce, water, vinegar, sesame oil, sesame seeds, sugar and ½ teaspoon garlic in small bowl. Set aside.
3. For waffles, whisk flour, cornstarch and salt in large bowl. Whisk in ice water and egg until combined. Fold in bell pepper, green onions, carrots and 2 teaspoons garlic.
4. Brush cooking grid of waffle maker with oil. Pour ½ cup batter onto center of waffle maker; gently spread to cover entire surface. Close lid; cook 2 minutes. Open lid; drizzle ½ teaspoon oil over top of waffle; close lid and continue cooking about 4 to 5 minutes or until golden brown and crisp.
5. Remove waffles to wire rack; keep warm. Repeat with remaining batter, brushing waffle maker with oil before each batch. Serve warm with dipping sauce.

Wasabi Salmon

makes 4 servings

2 tablespoons soy sauce

1½ teaspoons prepared wasabi paste, divided, plus additional to taste

4 salmon fillets with skin (6 ounces each)

¼ cup mayonnaise

1 Prepare grill or preheat broiler.

2 Combine soy sauce and ½ teaspoon wasabi paste in small bowl; mix well. Spoon mixture over salmon.

3 Place salmon, skin side down, on grid over medium heat or on rack of broiler pan. Grill or broil 4 to 5 inches from heat 8 minutes or until salmon is opaque in center.

4 Meanwhile, combine mayonnaise and remaining 1 teaspoon wasabi paste in small bowl; mix well. Taste and add more wasabi, if desired. Transfer salmon to serving plates; top with mayonnaise mixture.

Mu Shu Pork Wraps

makes 4 servings

- **1 tablespoon toasted sesame oil**
- **1 red bell pepper, cut into short, thin strips**
- **1 pork tenderloin (12 ounces), cut into strips**
- **1 medium zucchini or summer squash, or combination, cut into strips**
- **3 cloves garlic, minced**
- **2 cups prepared coleslaw mix or shredded cabbage**
- **2 tablespoons hoisin sauce**
- **¼ cup plum sauce**
- **4 (10-inch) whole wheat tortillas**

1 Heat oil in large deep nonstick skillet over medium-high heat. Add bell pepper; cook and stir 2 minutes. Add pork, zucchini and garlic; cook and stir 4 to 5 minutes or until pork is cooked through and vegetables are crisp-tender. Add coleslaw mix; cook and stir 2 minutes or until wilted. Add hoisin sauce; cook and stir 1 minute.

2 Spread plum sauce down centers of tortillas; top with pork mixture. Roll up tightly; cut diagonally in half.

Thai Chicken Pizza

makes 6 servings (2 pizzas)

Crust

1 package (¼ ounce) rapid-rise active dry yeast

1 teaspoon granulated sugar

1 cup warm water (120°F)

3 cups bread flour

2 tablespoons olive oil

1 teaspoon salt

Sauce

½ cup creamy peanut butter

½ cup hoisin sauce

2 tablespoons packed brown sugar

2 tablespoons toasted sesame oil

1 tablespoon minced fresh ginger

1 tablespoon water

1 tablespoon unseasoned rice vinegar

1 tablespoon soy sauce

2 cloves garlic, minced

1 teaspoon onion powder

1 teaspoon sriracha sauce

Topping

2 cups (8 ounces) shredded mozzarella cheese

1 cup chopped cooked chicken

4 green onions, thinly sliced

1 large carrot, julienned

½ cup bean sprouts

Chopped roasted peanuts and minced fresh cilantro

1 For crust, dissolve yeast and granulated sugar in warm water in large bowl of stand mixer. Let stand 5 minutes or until bubbly. Stir in flour, olive oil and salt until rough dough forms. Knead at low speed with dough hook 5 minutes or until dough is smooth and elastic. Shape dough into a ball. Place in large lightly greased bowl; turn to grease top. Cover and let rise in warm place about 1 hour or until doubled in size.

2 For sauce, combine peanut butter, hoisin sauce, brown sugar, sesame oil, ginger, 1 tablespoon water, vinegar, soy sauce, garlic, onion powder and sriracha in small saucepan. Cook over medium-low heat 3 to 5 minutes or until sauce is smooth and dark, whisking frequently. Remove from heat.

3 For topping, combine chicken and ½ cup sauce in medium skillet; cook and stir over medium heat 3 minutes or until chicken is glazed and heated through. Remove from heat.

4 Preheat oven to 500°F. Line two large baking sheets with parchment paper. Punch down dough; cut in half and shape into two balls. Cover and let rest 10 minutes. Roll out dough on lightly floured surface into two 12-inch circles. Spread ¼ cup sauce over each circle to within ½ inch of edge; sprinkle each pizza with ½ cup cheese. Top evenly with chicken, green onions, carrot and bean sprouts. Top with remaining cheese.

5 Bake 10 minutes or until crust is golden brown and cheese is melted. Sprinkle with peanuts and cilantro. Cut into wedges.

Index

Index

Index

Index

Metric Conversion Chart

VOLUME MEASUREMENTS (dry)

1/8 teaspoon = 0.5 mL
1/4 teaspoon = 1 mL
1/2 teaspoon = 2 mL
3/4 teaspoon = 4 mL
1 teaspoon = 5 mL
1 tablespoon = 15 mL
2 tablespoons = 30 mL
1/4 cup = 60 mL
1/3 cup = 75 mL
1/2 cup = 125 mL
2/3 cup = 150 mL
3/4 cup = 175 mL
1 cup = 250 mL
2 cups = 1 pint = 500 mL
3 cups = 750 mL
4 cups = 1 quart = 1 L

VOLUME MEASUREMENTS (fluid)

1 fluid ounce (2 tablespoons) = 30 mL
4 fluid ounces (1/2 cup) = 125 mL
8 fluid ounces (1 cup) = 250 mL
12 fluid ounces (1 1/2 cups) = 375 mL
16 fluid ounces (2 cups) = 500 mL

WEIGHTS (mass)

1/2 ounce = 15 g
1 ounce = 30 g
3 ounces = 90 g
4 ounces = 120 g
8 ounces = 225 g
10 ounces = 285 g
12 ounces = 360 g
16 ounces = 1 pound = 450 g

DIMENSIONS

1/16 inch = 2 mm
1/8 inch = 3 mm
1/4 inch = 6 mm
1/2 inch = 1.5 cm
3/4 inch = 2 cm
1 inch = 2.5 cm

OVEN TEMPERATURES

250°F = 120°C
275°F = 140°C
300°F = 150°C
325°F = 160°C
350°F = 180°C
375°F = 190°C
400°F = 200°C
425°F = 220°C
450°F = 230°C

BAKING PAN SIZES

Utensil	Size in Inches/Quarts	Metric Volume	Size in Centimeters
Baking or Cake Pan (square or rectangular)	8×8×2	2 L	20×20×5
	9×9×2	2.5 L	23×23×5
	12×8×2	3 L	30×20×5
	13×9×2	3.5 L	33×23×5
Loaf Pan	8×4×3	1.5 L	20×10×7
	9×5×3	2 L	23×13×7
Round Layer Cake Pan	8×1½	1.2 L	20×4
	9×1½	1.5 L	23×4
Pie Plate	8×1¼	750 mL	20×3
	9×1¼	1 L	23×3
Baking Dish or Casserole	1 quart	1 L	—
	1½ quart	1.5 L	—
	2 quart	2 L	—